SAM CHATER & LUCY MCCONAGHY

I0802173

SECONDARY ENGLISH IN ACTION

IN ACTION SERIES

A **WALKTHRUs** PRODUCTION

JOHN CATT
FROM HODDER EDUCATION

To order, please visit www.johncatt.com or contact Customer Service at education@hachette.co.uk / +44 (0)1235 827827.

ISBN: 978 1 9152 6186 1

First published in 2024 by
John Catt from Hodder Education,
An Hachette UK Company
15 Riduna Park, Station Road,
Melton, Woodbridge IP12 1QT
www.johncatt.com

The authorised representative in the EEA is Hachette Ireland, 8 Castlecourt Centre, Castleknock Road, Castleknock, Dublin 15, D15 YF6A, Ireland

Typeset in the UK.

Printed in the UK.

A catalogue record for this title is available from the British Library.

Cover illustration by Oliver Caviglioli

FSC www.fsc.org
MIX
Paper | Supporting responsible forestry
FSC™ C104740

CONTENTS

SERIES FOREWORD

This series of books was commissioned as a WalkThrus Production to complement two of our other series: The *Teaching Walkthrus*, Volumes 1, 2 and 3, and the *In Action* series. We believe that, together, they represent a powerful resource for teachers in schools and colleges in multiple subject settings.

The *In Action* series has proven to be very popular with busy teachers, enabling them to engage with a range of important ideas from cognitive science and from education research more generally. In each book, the authors explore the key ideas from a specific researcher, translating them into practical approaches that teachers can adopt in their practice. So far, the series includes:

- Rosenshine's Principles of Instruction
- Collins et al's Cognitive Apprenticeship
- Fiorella & Mayer's Generative Learning
- Shimamura's MARGE Model of Learning
- Sweller's Cognitive Load Theory
- Wiliam & Leahy's Five Formative Assessment Strategies
- Annie Murphy Paul's The Extended Mind
- Dunlosky's Strengthening the Student Toolbox
- Berger's An Ethic of Excellence
- Bjork & Bjork's Desirable Difficulties
- Ausubel's Meaningful Learning

Each of these books is a guide to interpreting the research in ways that can be applied in real-world classrooms. We have been delighted by the response to the series, with teachers telling us they value the brevity and clarity and the examples of theory in practice. It's so important for teachers to have a good grounding in cognitive science so that they have not only a clear model of how learning happens but also an understanding of all the potential barriers or difficulties that students experience. Bridging the gap between research and practice is a significant challenge because real-world classrooms are so much more complicated than the controlled conditions usually set up to investigate specific concepts in trials. The authors of the *In Action* books are all serving teachers or have taught in schools for many years, so their take on the theories and concepts that their books focus on is important and incredibly useful, grounded in the reality of teaching whole, complex classes.

It's by no means a comprehensive list – not yet – and we recognise that many other aspects of research would benefit from the same treatment. Books on Nuthall's Hidden Lives of Learners, Engelmann's ideas on direct instruction and Bandura's ideas on self-efficacy are all in the pipeline. We would also encourage every teacher to engage with Dan Willingham's *Why Don't Students Like School?*.

Released in parallel with the research-informed *In Action* series, our *Teaching WalkThrus* have also been popular with over 350,000 copies distributed across the three volumes. The idea of breaking ideas down into five-step visual guides, with short punchy descriptions, has proven very successful, allowing teachers to engage with a broad range of ideas in a very accessible format that informs their training, coaching or personal reflection. Significantly, *Teaching WalkThrus* were written in a style that is context free. They are generic in style so that teachers of all subjects in any setting can engage with them, transposing the ideas into their real-world contexts. The 150+ WalkThrus are organised into six main series, each of which represents an important area for professional learning:

Behaviour and relationships

- Lesson management
- Planning for good behaviour
- Positive correction
- Relationships and mindsets

Curriculum planning

- Assessment issues
- Broad design concepts
- Challenge, inclusion, diversity
- Detailed planning

Explaining and modelling

- Giving explanations and modelling
- Reading and writing
- Standards, expectations and scaffolding
- Types of explanations

Questioning and feedback

- Assessment
- Core questioning techniques
- Deeper questioning techniques
- Feedback

Practice and retrieval

- Guided to independent practice
- Reading
- Building fluency
- Retrieval practice
- Support and challenge

Mode B teaching

- Choices and creativity
- Making it real
- Oracy
- Student directed activities

With over 4000 schools having engaged with our online WalkThrus toolkit, we know that a great deal of valuable professional learning can be supported with our generic guides as a starting point. However, throughout each book we are at pains to stress the crucial need to adapt the ideas for specific circumstances. A five-step visual WalkThrus guide is not a set of rigid rules – it is a framework for thinking through an idea, deconstructing it so that teachers can then reconstruct it themselves, forming their own mental models for enacting powerful techniques in their own classrooms. That's the spirit.

Now, having explored research ideas in the *In Action* series and general pedagogical ideas in WalkThrus, we felt that the logical next step was to bring in subject-specific books in this new series, completing the third pillar of the trio: research, pedagogy, curriculum. Each book in the *In Action* subject series has been written by practising teachers who were tasked with presenting a summary of important ideas and debates from their subject to support busy teachers in their work. We have not imposed a rigid common format and our authors were encouraged to share their own perspectives with our readers. There is no definitive book on teaching science or history or maths or physical education – so these books are explicitly written with that in mind. The books represent the authors' personal perspective on how the ideas that circulate within each subject community can translate into great practice in the classroom. Once again, we invite readers to then adapt and adopt the ideas that make sense in their context.

I have to congratulate each author on their excellent work. It's daunting to summarise and capture the spirit of a subject, balancing depth of detail with sufficient breadth of coverage of content and related debates and implementation issues – all in what is meant to be a short book. If there is one thing that characterises all our books it is that they are accessible to teachers who are time poor. Each book in this series achieves that goal – they have an energy to them and a brilliant balance of rigour, steeped in experience with teaching the subject, alongside tons of examples to bring things to life.

We hope you find this book interesting and useful, adding an important dimension to your wider reading as a teacher doing the most important work there is: developing young people so that they have the knowledge, experience, confidence and wisdom they need to make sense of their world and play their part in the communities they belong to.

ABOUT THE AUTHORS

Sam Chater is an English teacher and assistant head at a secondary school in Stoke-on-Trent, who has vast experience in initial teacher education and staff development. His love of studying literature began with a BA (Hons) in English Literature, followed by an MA in Victorian Studies and an MPhil. His favourite texts to read are typically from the Victorian period or dystopian genre. He has since achieved the national professional headteacher qualification and has been a governor in a number of schools across the primary and secondary phase, while remaining extremely passionate about teaching the subject that he loves.

Lucy McConaghy is second in English at a secondary school in Stoke-on-Trent, as well as being the English subject lead and a subject mentor in initial teacher education and for early career teachers. Her BA (Hons) was in Anglo-Saxon, Norse and Celtic (an interdisciplinary study of history, literature and languages) and this combination underpins her historicist, connective approach and ongoing fascination with and passion for the study and development of both literature and languages across time. Lucy has since achieved an MBA and the national professional middle leader qualification as well as attaining Chartered Teacher status through the Chartered College of Teaching.

CHAPTER 1
VISION, TRADITION AND DEBATES

Vision

English is about communication, about narrative, about freedom and control, about manipulation and power. Fundamentally, at its heart, it is about exploring what it means to be human, to empathise in experiences and emotions across time and space, and to be able to communicate our own experiences and responses to those of others.

Our vision for the subject of English in secondary schools involves using the English language to interpret both oneself and the whole of society: in part through accessing a rich and diverse literary heritage; to make sense of, explore and question the wonderful complexities of the human psyche through the power of our always-changing, multi-cultural and ever-diversifying English language; to explore human relationships, human weaknesses, the way prejudice in its many forms can erode a society, and the power of language to manipulate and inspire, delude and delight, degrade and enlighten.

In short, English as a secondary school subject is always relevant to young people trying to navigate their way through an unstable and insecure modern world. Within this vision however, arguments about 'what English is' and 'whose English is it' perpetuate.

Traditions and debates

English as a taught school subject has always attracted controversy and been affected by political ideologies. Since the beginning of the 20th century, it is a subject dominated by broad oppositional shifts, from an early focus on literature (canon), to oracy and the uses of English in the 1970s and 1980s, shifting to a focus on writing and grammar in the late 1980s, through to the current 'knowledge-rich' perspective.

It is useful to trace some of the current debates within English back to the 1989 Cox report 'English for Ages 5 to 16' (Department of Education and Science, 1989). It is not atypical to see Cox's five views of English playing out in schools across the country, leading to questions about what the purpose(s) of English education is and who it is for.

- Personal growth view
- Cross-curricular view
- Adult needs view
- Cultural heritage view (appreciation of literature)
- Cultural analysis view (critical understanding of the world and the cultural environment)

Cox claimed that English teachers gave these views equal weight in the classroom, acknowledging the utilitarian nature of the subject but within a wider, creative and cultural frame. The Cox report also emphasised the subtlety of language acquisition and the multifarious purposes of the use of English, as well as the prominence and importance of wide reading and study of literature in developing language skills. Criticisms surround the report's monocultural emphasis and the National Curriculum Council shone a greater light on the importance of instruction in grammar, literacy (rather than oracy) and spelling. This focus has subsequently underpinned national curriculum requirements for English education.

These competing views of what English is and what it is for frame the ongoing debate about the respective values of skills and knowledge within the subject.

Skills or knowledge?

A. E. Housman famously claimed that 'all knowledge is precious whether or not it serves the slightest human use'. Current (and historic) debates on the teaching of secondary English centre around whether English is a knowledge-based subject, a skills-based subject, or a combination of the two – in something of an ouroboros cycle since, English has been considered as a school subject in its own right (Didau, 2021). This raises questions about how the sequencing of a curriculum, along with subject-specific pedagogy such as knowledge retrieval, interleaving and deliberate practice, allows students to know more, remember more and do more in each of the core concepts as well as to also experience the hinterland (Counsell, 2018) elements of English, such as the reading of a whole novel. Our own recent curriculum redesign, as well as collaboration with colleagues in schools across our region, draws on evidence from the research of writers such as Victoria Elliott, David Didau, Alex Quigley, the EEF and Doug Lemov.

What even is knowledge?

Elliot points to the difference between 'to know that' and 'to know how' or 'know when'. Some knowledge is factual, some of it is centred around processes (therefore skills?) and some of it is about critical evaluation (also skills?). Deborah Kidd (2018) meanwhile identifies that a 'rich curriculum moves way beyond knowledge. It moves towards the building upon knowledge to ensure that children know what to do with it. That they can't just name emperors and kings, but that they can consider the pitfalls of power. That they can't just name rivers and mountains, but that they understand how mankind is at the mercy of our natural environment as much as we are able to control aspects of it. They should understand that our capacity to destroy is matched by our capacity to create. They should know the best that has been said and done in a whole range of cultures as well as our own, but more than that – that the best that is to be said and done may well be yet to come. From them.'

Consequently, our view is that an English curriculum that values and finds a balance between both skills and knowledge must be the goal. Prioritising one over the other can create significant gaps in children's learning. In fact, as many commentators have observed, to pitch one approach over the other creates a 'false dichotomy' (Cornerstones Education, 2022); the two must go together.

Cultural capital versus diversity

David Didau's (2019) view of the 'value of cultural capital' – or 'cultural literacy' to use E. D. Hirsch Jr's term – is that it consists of knowledge that is useful for everyone to know. Being able to quote bits of Shakespeare or knowing who painted 'The Scream' may seem like trivia, but it enables us to access society in a way which would be impossible if we didn't know any of this. It's important *because* so many other people know it. If some people know something and others don't, those who don't will find themselves excluded or marginalised from the group that does.

So, should we teach the literary canon or not?

This is something of a moral dilemma within the teaching of English. Teach what students need to know to navigate the world and, subsequently, continue to privilege the works of the already privileged, powerful and dominant. Or don't, and instead teach writers and voices who speak directly to our students in voices that sound like their own, but potentially exclude them from that elitist world. Canonical knowledge is regularly condemned as 'stale, male and pale'. Instead of teaching the thoughts and works of the elite, shouldn't we instead prioritise the voices of the more marginalised?

This is a genuine problem. If we teach the works of the marginalised, people of colour, women, etc, this will not help students to understand why those works have not historically been part of the accepted canon, nor will it increase their cultural literacy.

If we teach both, the vision is that we provide access to some of that shared cultural knowledge that helps students navigate a world full of allusion, and also might allow them to begin developing the critical evaluative skills that will let them critique this world, to identify what is missing, to begin giving a voice to the dispossessed, the voiceless, and perhaps ultimately to change what that canon is. We see social justice and intellectual liberty as core aspects of the moral imperative of educators.

> *Yet all experience is an arch wherethro'*
>
> *Gleams that untravell'd world whose margin fades*
>
> *For ever and forever when I move. (Tennyson, 1842)*

Tennyson points to the quintessential problem of English teachers in making curriculum choices: the more we know about our own subject, the more there remains to know. There is a body of work that is continually being added to, and with that comes a seemingly almost infinite amount of choice. In the same way that many English teachers have probably been asked 'have you read this?' and when we haven't, get the response 'but you're an English teacher'. There is an assumption that we will have read every book, every poem, every play, every essay, every article that has ever been produced. We haven't. And within that, we cannot possibly share and choose to teach every single one of the texts we have ourselves read. As teachers, we must refine and choose and narrow down the breadth and richness of English literature to single texts or short extracts, keeping faithful to our vision of what English actually is.

Whether as classroom teachers or subject leaders, we have some control over decision making in our classrooms about what to teach and when, as well as pedagogy – do we teach components separately or together, for example?

How to counter this curriculum challenge

- Pair more 'canonical' texts with other voices, for example Edgar Allan Poe's *The Raven* alongside scripts from the TV series *Wednesday*. This then becomes a relevant and useful consideration of writers' choices of form in shaping meaning in texts, as well as the ongoing relevance of ideas and genres across time.
- Choose themes that can be explored across time, such as the concept of 'poetry of protest', which could start by examining the Romantics (canon) as proponents of protest through literature and art, through to the Harlem Renaissance, and the works of Dean Atta and Amanda Gorman, considering their shared choice of poetry as a way of expressing not dissimilar concerns about society through the ages.
- Seek ways to engage in the diversity of your own student body. In our school we have a reasonably large Filipino community, so to go alongside our study of Greek myths and legends (cultural capital), we also look at *Medusa* by Carol Ann Duffy and by Sylvia Plath (female perspective), and *Medusa* (in translation for our non-Tagalog speaking students) by Benilda Santos.
- There is no 'requirement' in terms of exam specifications for students to engage with literary criticism before A-level however, we believe that critical theory, adapted for students' ages, can be used as a lens for studying other texts that don't necessarily display modern social sensibilities. Obviously there is a need to adapt this to make it appropriate and accessible for the students you are teaching, but this could be giving one key sentence of an academic article to debate, or applying some critical perspectives to a text likely to be familiar to Key Stage 3 and 4 students (we have found the *Harry Potter* books to work well for this since it is ubiquitous, look at the appendices for more information).
- Staff openly discussing their own position in society: 'Atta seems to be suggesting that … I can empathise with this point of view because … however, I can't fully identify because my own lived experience is as a white person…'. Remind students of the inordinate power of literature to help us see, empathise, experience and through the imagination live the lives of other people.

Taking these practical strategies into consideration, we must remember that time needs to be given for reflection on and refinement of the curriculum. This could include sharing of resources as well as student voice. Using the example of the increasing Filipino community in our own school, leaders need to be aware of changes not only in pupil intake but also in staff make-up. Staff can play an important role in bringing different experiences and viewpoints to the classroom.

The skillset of English teachers

Anecdotally, teachers of English in secondary schools are more likely to hold a degree in English literature than in English language or an associated subject, such as creative writing, media, journalism, etc. This has an implication for teaching – is English even a homogenous subject at all if it can be divided into these separate disciplines at university level?

While most of us feel that we are teaching things not within our specific specialism at times (since what can be considered to comprise 'English' is so vast), there is also a relevant consideration in terms of whether literature specialists really feel empowered to teach creative writing (genuinely as a subject in its own right rather than simply to meet a set of artificial exam criteria), or if someone whose degree is in writing feels equally empowered when faced with teaching literature without the schema developed by someone who has studied, for example, multiple Shakespeare plays or Victorian literature in units at university.

The answer to this perhaps lies in a couple of key areas, the first being teacher self-awareness and self-reflection, with a view to ongoing CPD. Due to the nature of the subject and teacher specialisms however, CPD for English teachers should be individual and tailored. While this does not always occur in the context of whole school development, as individuals we absolutely can take ownership of filling some of the gaps in our own knowledge. The second area is in collaboration within our departments and both across local schools and nationally. As John Donne famously put it, 'No man is an island entire of itself', and neither is any English teacher. Nor are we individually experts in everything, but across the breadth of the country is a huge amount of expertise. Consequently, we would urge teachers to participate in and pursue opportunities for collaboration, with colleagues and in wider CPD and professional association networks nationally.

A subject in crisis? Problems facing English

Recent figures show that between 2016–17 and 2020–21 there has been a national decline of 25% in students taking English literature A-level, with a corresponding drop of 20% for English language. Since 2016, there has been a 23% decline in female students taking English subjects at A-level, increasing to a 34% decline in male students (Education Data Lab, n.d. a; Education Data Lab, n.d. b). It seems evident from research by the British Academy (Hopkins et al., 2023) that the uptake from A-level to degree level in English remains broadly consistent; enrolments for literature in universities are down around 8–9% as a consequence of the falling numbers taking the subject at A-level rather than any change in conversion rates between further and higher education.

Why is this?

Challenges

There is a widespread perception that the current (at time of writing) GCSE syllabus in England (2015 onwards) is dry and test-focused, with learning by rote, which has put students off pursuing the subject further. The focus of students, caregivers and even some schools on achieving a grade 4 or 5 to continue to further post-16 education (the grade varies depending on setting) means that students often see English language as a gateway to other subjects rather than a subject worth studying in its own right. This has a knock-on effect for teachers of English who are pressured to meet targets and treat exams as exercises in hoop-jumping, quickly learning tricks to adapt to new assessments. But these tricks are not 'English', or at least not what it can and should be.

There has also been a narrowing of the literature curriculum and much less time and opportunity to teach beyond set texts. In some areas, Ofsted produces pressure for uniformity, assessing 'typicality and sequence', which places limits on teaching content and activity. There is clearly a shared perceived narrowing of what constitutes English in recent years, and this is impacting the ongoing uptake of our subject at a higher level after it is no longer compulsory. It begs questions about whether the current GCSE framework, in English language in particular, is in fact fit for purpose.

GCSE English language, as Nicholls (2022) says, 'is the piece of paper a person must hold to show that they can access spoken and written materials and make sense of the world on the next phase of their journey to becoming fully fledged citizens of the world. And it is proof that a person can effectively access any other part of the curriculum and indeed communicate their own understanding and knowledge about – well – everything.'

So, in our view, what's missing in English language GCSE? Any discussion should include learning about spoken language and the continuing evolution of English. English is a living evolving thing that connects in its diversity, it amuses and delights. Students should learn about debates over 'political correctness' and the power of language to influence, as well as sociolinguistic, cultural and historic aspects to communication. It should include discussion and debate around evolving forms of communication, including modern communication.

To 'increase standards', the 'new' GCSEs of 2015 have largely removed any teaching of media, yet there is a huge need for students to learn about such a large aspect of their current and likely-to-be future lives, teaching critical evaluation and thinking. In a real world needs model, for students, there is less benefit in being able to read a Victorian article about travelling by the newly-invented bicycle than there is in being able to analyse use of presentational devices in a party political election leaflet. Although some cynics may argue that perhaps this is the point! Studying Victorian writing is important within a cultural heritage and cultural literacy context and we would never deny this. However, this works within the context of literature, not as language study, unless it is part of a relevant dialogue about our changing language over time, which also considers aspects of dialect, accent and sociolect within a debate about standard English, privilege and prejudice.

'In English Language, students should be demonstrating that they can appreciate the difference between an email and a letter in terms of mode and context. They should know all about algorithms and news feeds – advertising, memes, social media – and should be competent in their ability to check sources and account for crucial aspects of context which are critical to the reader's full understanding of a text. They should be aware of audience positioning and the tricks of the trade such as image manipulation and captioning so that they can filter and process the information which will bombard them throughout their lives. They should be able to debate, thoughtfully and analytically, issues about language which demonstrate both its power and importance. Ultimately, they should be empowered as both consumers and producers of language' (Nicholls, 2022).

Tackling this as part of curriculum design

This is easy enough at Key Stage 3 where there is more freedom to explore. However, a GCSE specification that requires students to write in a completely artificial way, producing a short story, newspaper article or speech in 45 minutes with no access to research or tools that any writer in the real world would naturally use, such as a thesaurus, is not a real reflection of writing in practice and the artificiality of this does not necessarily help students learn how to write 'properly' in a way that might be transferable to writing in the real world.

In order to attempt to ensure students receive their 'passport' to the world beyond, teachers understandably teach their students to jump through hoops, learning almost by rote sentence structures and mnemonics for techniques (DAFOREST OR SHAMPOO anyone?) that students can replicate in an exam to access levels on the mark scheme. There is very little genuine writing or writing practice that occurs. There is little teaching time given (because little time is available) to consideration of the real, fundamental differences in written form. It requires an immense amount of courage and faith that teaching your Key Stage 4 students real journalistic writing and methods will enable them to produce the kind of piece that will receive high marks in a GCSE exam.

We're with Jennifer Webb (2020) when she says, 'everyone has a right to write. An inalienable right, as an art form.' This means changing our philosophy on writing right the way through the secondary curriculum. Write less, but more meaningfully. It's not about output but about crafting, to really understand form, language choices, style, voice, tone. And editing, revisiting, drafting, not within a single lesson or just the next one but over time.

There are also specific challenges in English related to male students. There is a widely shared view that English is 'not for boys'. Pinkett and Roberts (2019) talk about 'the engagement myth' that – amongst other things – results in reinforcing potentially harmful stereotypes about gender and encourages low expectations of boys. The researchers remind us that 'teach boys in exactly the same way that you teach girls (or all students). High challenge. High expectations. No gimmicks. No shortcuts.' And we need to remember this when planning and delivering the English curriculum. Can you imagine if someone were to say, 'we've chosen A Midsummer Night's Dream to read in order to engage our female students who just want to read about romance, plus girls like fairies and animals too'? We should choose Macbeth because it's an incredibly good play written in the most emotive and powerful verse, showcasing some important ideas about morality and power, not because it's violent and bloody and boys like that sort of stuff. Does it make girls who appreciate Macbeth masculine? This is not to say that texts that raise questions and discussion about gender have no place in the curriculum. They absolutely do if English is to fulfil its role in getting young people to consider people and their societies. It is stereotypes that have no place in the curriculum.

A basic sense of reading for pleasure and finding enjoyment in cultural activities related to reading and writing is also disappearing. There may be many reasons for this including: few or no books owned at home; limited access to libraries but also online resources behind paywalls; for A-level students the pressure to work which means there is not time to read outside that spent on study. It is also the case that some young people see their engagement in areas such as fan fiction, blogging, YouTubing, gaming, and animation as distinct from anything they study in English at school, which in part links back to this sense of narrowing what English is, can, should be all about.

Do we also need to address the question: 'What is literature?' Are Shakespeare's plays literature but young adult fiction not? If English literature teaches students to critically analyse 'texts', then how far do film and media fit into our broader definitions of what constitutes a text? There is a problem in challenging perceptions about the narrowness of the subject in these regards, especially at Key Stages 3 and particularly 4 (although arguably less so at A-level).

Perhaps the biggest hurdle we face is a cultural one based around current narratives and assumptions about careers and skills. The emphasis on STEM subjects within schools, colleges and in much of the media, particularly when it comes to careers advice, has seen English routinely undervalued. It is often viewed as a subject where the benefits are vague and amongst the higher education community there is a concern that this could lead to a position where the need to secure a good job means English (and arts and humanities subjects more broadly) becomes a luxury subject and the province of the privileged (Hopkins et al., 2023). Students are dissuaded from studying subjects they genuinely enjoy and value on a personal level (which obviously extends beyond English to most arts and humanities subjects) because there is a narrative that this will leave them unemployable and destitute.

To counter the problem, English teachers need to challenge these assumptions directly in the classroom. They will need to weave employment through the curriculum with useful information about what career paths are possible, what they entail, and their associated incomes and market information. This should help to demonstrate to young people that careers which at least provide sufficient income to pay the mortgage are valid choices from English, as well as promoting elements of job satisfaction that are not financially motivated – an area we see as sometimes lacking in student perceptions of careers. See the section on 'promoting english' on page 119 for some further practical suggestions to tackle this.

What does all this mean for subject leaders and teachers?

- Curriculum design: English departments need a **clear vision** of what studying English is for them, with key essential ingredients that are obvious in all areas of the intended curriculum.
- Commonality of English literature: an exploration of what it means to be human, coupled with an examination of how this has been expressed by societies over time, and how language has developed as a result of the changing world.

A department could consider a curriculum linked through:

- How people use power
- Humans as explorers and creators
- Human relationships
- David Didau (2023) has also kindly shared a curriculum via his website www.learningspy.co.uk/english-gcse/oat-english-curriculum/.

Our approach to the curriculum also includes 'big questions' that direct the department to the key thinking that we want students to undertake, exploring what it means to be human and exist in this world, at some point in time.

Our curriculum example

Whilst we would by no means present this as an ideal or perfect curriculum, the following section is an overview of the current English curriculum at our setting, with some justifications to our curriculum choices. Our curriculum is backwards engineered from Key Stage 4 where text choices are governed by exam board specifications. Literature texts are all linked through a theme of power, from poetry to the power of economics in *A Christmas Carol*, questions about leadership, ambition and care for one's people in both *Macbeth* and *Lord of the Flies*, and power of personal choice and free will running through all of them. Having made these text choices, we then designed a Key Stage 3 curriculum to consider similar themes and ideas, often from a different perspective and incorporating a wider range of voices across time and forms of writing than we are always able to at Key Stage 4.

Key Stage 3

Threads of power, conflict, morality, greed and injustice weave together a range of diverse texts, writers and language from ancient Greece to the modern day, across the whole of our Key Stage 3 and 4 curriculum. A thematic approach to our Year 7 curriculum allows students to experience a journey of sea travel, heroism and the telling of stories, from Greek myth and drama through to the comedies and tragedies of Shakespeare's Elizabethan England, consider morality in *Treasure Island*, the chaotic streets of London during the 2011 riots and the coming to light of the Windrush scandal in 2018. A focus on narratives and voice allows a consideration of how stories are told, and told 'slant', in order for students to then consider whose voices are marginalised and through their own narratives allow those voices to speak.

A contextual approach to the Year 8 curriculum means an in-depth study of the Victorian psyche, through to Gothic literature and non-fiction. We track the growth of Gothic fiction from rural to urban and then to American short stories and poetry (eventually linking to the development of dystopian literature in Year 9), as well as the use of Gothic tropes in modern TV dramas. Students revisit the conflict of Shakespeare's England through *Romeo and Juliet* to *Noughts and Crosses*, continuing this thread of conflict into poetry (Renaissance, Enlightenment and Emancipation, looking at diverse voices in poetry across time).

The Year 9 curriculum acts as a bridge to help prepare students for the challenges of the GCSE curriculum: students encounter literature that has been selected to inspire their growing minds and to compliment the skill sets that they have developed. To build understanding of allegory before diving into two texts at GCSE – *A Christmas Carol* and *Lord of the Flies* – students grow their knowledge of the dystopian genre through a range of extracts and forms, including dystopian graphic novels and TV scripts, before whole text study of *Animal Farm*. Allegorical contexts continue through study of the play *The Crucible* expanding ideas about power and witchcraft before tackling *Macbeth* at GCSE. Students finish the year by continuing their consideration of poetry across time by exploring ideas about power and protest, from the Romantics and American civil rights writing to contemporary writers, such as Amanda Gorman and Warsan Shire.

So, what is English made of?

In our view core concepts of English consist of:

- Narrative
- Form
- Oracy
- Interpreting texts
- Creating texts
- Grammar and the structure of language

CHAPTER 2
TEACHING ORACY

In the opening chapter, we defined the study of English as one about communication, narrative, freedom and control, and manipulation and power. At its heart, fundamentally, it is about exploring what it means to be human, to empathise in experiences and emotions across time and space, and being able to communicate our own experiences and our responses to those of others. It is worthwhile to reiterate this vision of the subject at this point to reinforce the importance of teaching oracy, an aspect that realistically (and unfortunately) can fall by the wayside in English classrooms. When something is not valued at the level of assessments on which schools are judged (GCSEs), it is a brave decision to invest significant time into something that may well develop students on a personal level but will not have any bearing on how the school is deemed to have performed.

Much like reading and writing, teaching oracy is not the sole responsibility of the English teacher, but the English classroom does give wonderfully rich opportunities for students to improve their oracy skills, as well as using oracy to improve their knowledge of other aspects of English. In fact, it is the inherent nature of English to consider ideas and responses orally. The difficulty is in scaffolding and developing this, rather than it simply encompassing everything that naturally takes place in the classroom anyway. We also need to remember that children's language develops orally initially; they learn language through listening first and then mimicking until they can speak. Hart and Risley's 1995 research discovered that by the time they reached school, children from a word-rich home were likely to have encountered 30 million more words than those from a more disadvantaged background. Much work has since centred around this vocabulary gap, for example by Alex Quigley, and so the gap in what is spoken to and heard by children from birth ultimately has an impact on how well students can eventually read and write.

A fundamental challenge with teaching oracy is in defining what it does and does not encompass, otherwise there is a danger that it ends up covering all 'talk' that happens within a classroom setting, in a similar vein to how literacy education involves focused attention on specific strands to develop skills and understanding in reading and writing rather than simply any activity that might take place with a pen in hand. Alexander's definition is perhaps helpful here: '[Oracy] is what the school does to support the development of children's capacity to use speech to express their thoughts and communicate with others, in education and in life.' It is therefore related to concrete teaching strategies and not simply 'classroom talk' unless this is structured. We would suggest four different strands in approaching development of oracy skills: accountable talk, exploratory talk, dialogic talk and presentational talk.

Structured talk in the English classroom

Recommendation six of the EEF's *Improving Literacy in Secondary Schools* (2021a) research provides four key recommendations around providing opportunities for structured talk:

- Talk matters both in its own right and because of its impact on other aspects of learning.
- High quality talk is typically well-structured and guided by teachers.
- Accountable talk is a useful framework to ensure talk is high quality, and it emphasises how talk can be subject specific.
- Teachers can support students by modelling high quality talk, for example including key vocabulary and metacognitive reflection.

Despite the intrinsic nature of talking, this research demonstrates the need for the teacher's input to be substantial in terms of teaching oracy. But how many English teachers honestly prioritise oracy as a core concept of the subject? We debated where this section should feature in this book, with it near the end at one point, before eventually deciding that early discussion of oracy might reinforce its importance and begin to seek to redress oracy being somewhat overlooked in the classroom. Chapter 4: Interpreting texts also highlights the benefits of oracy in the English classroom in relation to building schema and avoiding extraneous cognitive load, and of the need to encourage improved prosody for students reading.

If you can say it, you can write it

David Didau (2014) asserts that 'if you can say it, you can write it'. However, many – if not all – English teachers will probably have come across the student who is articulate, eloquent and can express their ideas perceptively and sensitively when speaking, but then has a shock the first time they read something this student has written because it appears to have been composed by a different human being. There can be a vast gap between oral and written expression (in either direction). As Latham (2002) indicates, 'spoken language forms a constraint, a ceiling not only on the ability to comprehend but on the ability to write, beyond which literacy cannot progress'.

Didau's logic follows a 'think-say-write' pattern. Obviously thinking must come first since nothing can be written or should be said if it has not been thought about first. He also points to the issue of how difficult it is to track what someone thinks in the classroom. Teachers can only judge the output of thought through speech or writing; writing has its own inherent challenges and approaches. Speech is more immediately measurable.

Is the 'thinking' part where some problems lie in English?

The problem with getting students to write analytical PEE/WHW-type paragraphs, for example, is often in students knowing what point they wish to make. You can teach a student strategies to identify quotations to evidence their points, to name and pick out literary and linguistic techniques, but actually being able to independently identify that Miller's use of the 16th century setting of Salem in *The Crucible* is an allegorical criticism of 1960s anti-communist America is a much higher order thinking skill than being able to identify that he uses a metaphor when he says that 'the little crazy children are jangling the keys to the kingdom'.

We also need to consider the contexts of producing spoken rather than written texts. Spoken language is usually context-bounded as a specific discourse event which makes immediate sense to those present (and does not necessarily when viewed exophorically and asynchronously), whereas there is a need in writing to make the reader aware of contextual factors that are more likely to be apparent to oral participants. Speech is live, real-time, involving audience participation and prosody to convey meanings, therefore a speaker can modify what they say if the audience appears confused; this is an affordance of speech which constrains the written word.

Fluency: the problem with 'if you can say it, you can write it'

Fluency in the physical element of writing is imperative as it can prevent clarity in expression and delay thinking time so that an idea can be lost before being fully committed to paper. If the fluency and speed in getting ideas down is not there, then it doesn't matter if you can say it because you won't be able to physically write it before you forget what it is that you wanted to write.

So, if writing follows speech which follows thought, how do we effectively develop structured talk in the English classroom?

Reframing

To address the need for accuracy and precision to communicate ideas orally, editing and redrafting are just as important stages as when writing. Focus on rephrasing or reframing speech so we edit it at this point (before reaching any writing frame) – we should encourage our students to aim to speak like an essay. Students are also more likely to remove unnecessary frames from their speech as they can hear repetition and clunkiness naturally once we begin to direct conscious attention to it.

Teacher: How does Macbeth feel when he says 'full of scorpions is my mind dear wife'?

Student 1: Tortured

Teacher: Great, now rephrase that as a full sentence – make sure you use 'because' to explain your thinking.

Student 1: In this line Macbeth feels tortured because he refers to scorpions in his mind, which would feel really painful, like you were a victim of torture.

Teacher: Excellent! Student 2, could you give us a version that uses some relevant subject terminology now?

Student 2: In this line Macbeth feels tortured because he uses the metaphor of scorpions in his mind, which would feel really painful, like you were a victim of torture.

Teacher: Amazing. Now, Student 3, can you repeat what they've already said, but also add in what Shakespeare intends the effect of this to be on the audience?

Student 3: In this line Macbeth feels tortured because he uses the metaphor of scorpions in his mind, which would feel really painful, like you were a victim of torture. Shakespeare intends us to empathise with Macbeth here because he is in torment over his guilt.

From the students' point of view, it is important for accountability that they perceive this as cold calling with no idea who will be called upon to answer however, from the teacher's perspective, this may need to be targeted towards students you know will be able to develop the point, perhaps from earlier discussion with them or your own awareness and assessment of which student can add in the detail needed, especially in Student 3's role!

Suggested structures for speech:

- This might mean… because…
- The writer used the phrase… to imply…
- The writer's intention is…
- This could also suggest…
- The word … is effective because…

Displaying academic vocabulary on the board during oral tasks also sets an expectation that students will use it, as well as having examples in exercise books that we guide students to.

Oral vocabulary instruction

As Neuman and Wright (2014) point out, students need to hear a new word, and they need multiple opportunities to say it themselves. Their research suggests that 24 repetitions are required for 80% of children to successfully remember a word. Once again, this has implications for the teaching of key vocabulary, but perhaps English teachers could take a leaf out of the MFL classroom where rote pronunciation, even as a whole class, can be a common successful strategy.

Accountable talk

Making students accountable for everything they do (or do not do) in the classroom is an essential element of behaviour management and setting of expectations. It needs to be considered as part of oracy instruction otherwise certain students will dominate group or class discussions, some will be ignored and overlooked, and the whole discussion will crumble into pointlessness. Strategies here are nothing startlingly innovative or new, although they are helpful in ensuring that students remain accountable whilst having smaller scale discussions. However, we would stress that oracy is about more than simply accountability for what is spoken and by whom. In class discussion, there is a need to pose questions and then pause to give thinking time for all students. Cold calling sets an expectation that all students might be called in to respond, so all will think of an answer without scope for opting out. Probing questioning is necessary to draw out and develop whole class discussion. At the end, it is important to get students to summarise and record the conversation.

- Think pair share and Rally Robin: be explicit about turn taking and expectations for all students doing something during a task (e.g. noting what each student offers in turn).
- Questioning could alternate between 'what did your partner say?' and 'what did you say?'
- Use frames to scaffold talk and develop student responses, for example use the format: 'On one hand, Macbeth is influenced by the witches because ... but on the other hand ...'

Exploratory talk

Exploratory talk is where students listen critically and constructively to each other's ideas to reach an overall agreement on a topic. Essential to this is a dilemma type question that eschews simplistic responses.

- What words might you use to describe the central character? Think of three each, share them and decide the best ones.
- To what extent do you think Shakespeare intends the audience to believe Macbeth is acting of his own free will? You should consider the influence of the witches, Lady Macbeth, Macbeth's own stated desires, and Elizabethan ideas about fate and fortune.
- Which ghost has the greatest impact on Scrooge's eventual transformation? Explain your reasoning.

Scaffolds to support

Students need models here to help with ways of probing and disagreeing without being argumentative:

- Have we missed anything here?
- That is an interesting point. Have you considered that...
- What other conclusions might somebody draw from this?
- Is it possible that...
- I may be wrong, but what I think you are saying is...
- If this, then... if that, then...

- Have we thought about everything... Let's check we considered...
- In summary...

Dialogic talk

The aim of dialogic talk is to develop students' abilities to discuss, extend and evaluate their own thinking skills. As Socrates said, it is about getting people to ask better questions as an iterative dialectic process. It needs to be clear to students when this type of talk is taking place that the goal is not winning an argument, but collaboratively finding understanding, knowledge and truth. It is about getting to the heart of an idea together.

Dialogic questions (these are more open than exploratory questions that have a specific learning intention):

- What do you mean by that?
- Why do you think that's true?
- What are other ways we could approach this problem?
- Are there any strong counterarguments to this?
- Can you help me understand how you came to that conclusion?
- If we did this/considered this from another viewpoint, what material impact would it have on our argument/beliefs/thoughts/ideas?

Particularly with older students, it can also be worth introducing them to the concepts of Socratic process in discussion. This does not necessarily need to be framed as a full Socratic debate, with inner and outer circles of participants and viewers, but the principles and particularly a focus on reflection, clarification and refinement of ideas. It takes time to embed this and needs to be modelled and coached, but it gives students a clear frame for discussion and ensures the listener remains accountable throughout.

1. **Receive**: really listen to the other person's view, without judgement, disagreement or prejudice.
2. **Reflect**: sum up the other person's viewpoint and reflect it back to them. Clarify anything that you are not clear about.
3. **Refine**: ask them to provide their evidence. Discover why they think what they think – discover facts, beliefs and assumptions that underpin their standpoint. Challenge assumptions to test their validity.

4. **Restate**: original speaker reformulates or restates their position, taking into consideration any new learning or change resulting from the previous stages. Adapt or renew wording.
5. **Repeat**: now they have a new viewpoint, go back to the start and work through the cycle again. Challenge new assumptions.

We can also offer our students the magic of 'because', 'but', 'so' and 'however'. In many ways, the simplicity of the words helps students to remember them as a strategy; teachers can insist that students add one of these at the end of any idea to keep developing it until they cannot add any more!

Presentational talk

This is perhaps what some people mean by oracy, when commenting that their students' oracy skills are sub-par. Presentational talk has more in common with writing than speech, and in fact is usually underpinned by an earlier written text to allow structuring of complex ideas, presentational devices, features of rhetoric, a more sophisticated lexis than is typically employed in everyday talk. Writing involves complex thought, which can be more abstract, impersonal, objective, detached. Written language allows analytical and abstract thought – if you can't write it, you also cannot think or say it.

We therefore need to be clear with our students about the purpose of 'talk': are we asking them to create, consider, discuss and evaluate ideas, or do we want them to move to a stage beyond this where they then present them?

In our view it would be better to teach presentational type talk as something more akin to writing; a piece which is first written, redrafted, edited, perfected, including a range of appropriate devices – and then has prosodic skills practiced as a performance piece. The section on 'Write like a speech writer' has more specific advice for developing these skills.

Finally, it is worth mentioning oral fluency skills in reading aloud. Fluency can be supported by activities such as choral speaking, where students read together, or echo reading, where a stronger reader (a good student or adult in the room) reads first and then students repeat. The significant thing here is that for this to have any impact on improving fluency in reading aloud, multiple re-readings and repetition of any text is essential.

CHAPTER 3
MAKING MEANING

Before delving into any detail on teaching elements of English such as reading, writing, grammar or oracy, teachers need to consider holistically how students are going to gain an appreciation of how writers create meanings. Perhaps the granularity of analytical questions in English language at GCSE, and predominantly extract-based approaches to English literature, coupled with a perceived need to 'teach to the test' can mean that English in the classroom can become bogged down in details. Of course, those details – the connotations of words, patterns in texts, similes and pronouns and punctuation marks – are incredibly important in shaping meaning but so is the larger picture, which is perhaps what we can overlook. Consequently, we suggest considering two aspects of how writers shape meanings through their choices at this 'big picture' level before we dive into an examination of the specifics and minutiae of a text: narrative and form.

Narrative

Narrative is the fundamental lens through which humans make sense of the world: 'without narrative there would be little way for us to make meaning of our experiences' (Didau, 2021b). Narrative does not just shape fiction but characterises much human communication and attempts to make sense of and rationalise the chaos of the world around us, to attempt to provide meaning in everything. As Didau (2021c) points out, we 'tend to conform to particular ways of structuring our stories – chronology, climaxes, resolutions – and by doing so we make it easier for those around us to understand our experiences'. Much storytelling is underpinned by the principle of causality: in a search for meaning, we tend to apply cause and effect thinking to make sense of sometimes unconnected random occurrences. The role of the narrator is also paramount and students need to be aware of the idea that everyone 'tells it slant', biased towards their own world view, experiences, desires and goals. Together, this means that much of human communication can be characterised as storytelling, but storytelling is a truth rather than the truth.

Frameworks through which to view narratives can help to support student understanding. Whilst both Aristotle and Freytag's models were designed for drama, they can also (at least in part) be applied to the plot of prose narratives. Unpicking this, and perhaps where writers deviate from this frame and discussing why and the impact on the reader, can aid learning, looking perhaps at non-chronological structures.

Components of plot:

- Beginning: inciting moment which sets in motion other events
- Complication
- Middle: a turning point
- Denouement or unravelling of the plot
- End: a moment of final surprise or sense of resolution

Story models

Although academics have argued about exactly how many story models there are (for example Booker's [2005] 7 archetypes), we believe it is useful to teach students about narrative models and get them to apply stories they already know to these. These can then be used as a frame for deconstructing future narratives and for students to construct their own. For example:

- Overcoming the monster
- Rags to riches
- The quest
- Voyage and return
- The rebirth
- Comedy (as per Aristotle, characters are presented as worse than they are in life, and the fundamentals of the plot are about order being resolved from chaos)
- Tragedy (in the Aristotelian mould, characters are presented as better than they are in life, and the plot is all about causation)

It might help students to comprehend the assertion that narrative archetypes tend to underpin human communication by applying these to some other familiar, real world scenarios, for example:

- Overcoming the monster: finding a vaccination for Covid.

- Rags to riches: the autobiographies of many business people and often sportspeople as well, for example, Lewis Hamilton, Marcus Rashford, Alan Sugar.
- Voyage and return: the expeditions of people such as Charles Darwin or Ernest Shackleton.

If we view these as narrative archetypes, this might help students to begin to understand and, subsequently, analyse the way components of those archetypes are put to work in different scenarios, for example to explain the drama and hyperbole of a news report or the structure and chronology of a science article. The significance of narrative in constructing meaning is acknowledged by non-fiction writers as well. Paul Smith's 2021 book on acquiring wealth through property investment, *Wealth Through Property,* (snooped on in a moment of nosiness about other traveller's reading choices on a plane) begins with him stating that he is 'your storyteller and educator' for this process.

Jacob Ross suggests an alternative archetypal frame for short stories:

- Encounter stories: the protagonist encounters something out of the ordinary that shakes up their daily routine.
- Classic stories: the protagonist defeats their antagonist after a period of struggle.
- Self-realisation stories: the protagonist learns something about themselves, the world or other people.
- The isolated moment: its intensity and impact on the teller.
- Parabolic stories: those stories imbued with layers of symbolism and meaning, allegorical tales.

As Ross (2020) points out, any story can contain elements of each of these, but the key to the type of story 'becomes evident by what the writer chooses to emphasise and amplify'.

Whichever archetype model you choose to follow, this is a particularly important message in the classroom when we are teaching story archetypes as students need to understand that a significant part of a writer's craft is in this nuanced emphasis rather than perceiving something like narrative as a purely binary choice. Questioning and discussing with students where a text does and does not fit into story moulds is therefore an inherently valuable and necessary activity, especially when extended by considering why the writer has made this decision and what the impact on the reader is.

Construction of narrative

As students gain a greater understanding of narrative framing, we can also help them to view reading as an act of construction in itself, to go beyond the clichéd 'there are no wrong answers in English'. Whilst we do not necessarily need to go full on Barthes and Rosenblatt and announce the death of the author (a more moderate approach that views the significance of a writer's choices through the lens of impact on individual readers has more relevance to our students and the way in which they are assessed; we can save the nuances and full detangling of literary criticism for university), a brief introduction to the principles of reader response theory can begin to make the process of unpicking our deconstruction of writer's choices, and the conditionality inherent in the reconstruction of meaning from these.

Questions to aid this might include:

- What is the narrative structure of the text?
- How has the writer chosen to present the chronology? How does this shape our understanding of what is going on, e.g. retrospective re-evaluation, hindsight, immediacy of action to build tension.
- Who are we positioned with? How?
- Are we close to the action or at a distance?
- Is it omniscient or personal?
- How does this shape our understanding and interpretation of events along with the characters?
- Who are we positioned with and against?
- If our positioning as a reader were different, who would we sympathise with? How would it change our knowledge and understanding of plot events?

Retelling/adaptation/version

Firstly, adaptation of existing narrative is a metacognitive process that evidences and extends students' comprehension of and thinking about a story. It requires understanding of the building blocks of narrative, and especially of the significance of narrative voice in shaping and shifting meaning. Subsequently, getting students to reflect on their own work and retelling from a different perspective as an act of writing and construction can also enhance their conscious understanding of what can be unconscious automated choices to focus on their own intended effects. This allows them to edit, redraft and create better texts and has the added advantage of getting them to overtly focus on the idea of conscious intentional decision-making in the construction of texts. See the writing section on page 96 for further discussion of use of commentary on writing as metacognitive reflection on the writing process.

Adaptation can sometimes also get over the blank page problem since there is already a story there to be told, and so students can then focus on their own crafting of a text rather than having to invent and imagine character, settings and plots.

SOLO taxonomy (Biggs and Collis, 1982) appears to have rather fallen out of fashion in educational pedagogy in recent ideas, but there is something in the idea that being able to create something new from what you know is evidence of strong knowledge and understanding of the original text and the writer's craft in constructing it and requires this basis to underpin it. This runs alongside the knowledge and skills debate in English; knowledge must precede and underpin skills, otherwise 'the "skills based" approach bounces off them [students], it's like trying to build on sand' (Didau, 2018).

In our school, we have chosen for Year 7 to begin their secondary school journey with a focus on narratives. This includes stories that have perpetuated across time – myths and legends – and the retelling that has become an almost equally fundamental part of those stories. Dealing with archaic stories means that factual historical truth is at best murky and probably unobtainable. This then allows us, in the classroom, to focus on the human truths that are being told – to look at similarities, differences and writer's choices in versions and retellings of the story, and then finally, for the students to tell it again themselves.

We have scaffolded this by looking at several different versions of the same narrative, for example, the tale of Medusa in Greek mythology, but retold from several angles and looking at different forms – both prose narrative and poetry. This has also presented an opportunity to look at retellings from different perspectives and viewpoints, allowing students to hear diverse voices and versions.

Form

Even before narrative, a writer's choice of form is perhaps their first choice in terms of shaping meaning. They are cueing us in to all the conventions of those texts, which lend shape, coherence and indeed some meaning to a text before anything else is added by a writer. Someone has chosen to write a sonnet, knowing all about sonnet form, therefore they either want to say something about some form of love, drawing on all the literary tradition that sonnets give, or they want us to think that's what they are doing so they can then subvert this to say something else. There is already meaning inherent in this choice.

Similarly, we could infer from a writer's decision to write an allegorical novel that they want the reader to have to work at deciphering the meaning. There might be a certain level of challenge in this that could potentially obscure meaning to an extent at the outset (in opposition to writing a newspaper article on the same topic where the primary goal would be clarity), but once uncovered, that meaning would remain with the reader potentially for a lifetime. Novels such as *Lord of the Flies*, *A Christmas Carol*, *Animal Farm*, *An Inspector Calls*, *To Kill a Mockingbird*, are often said to have shaped people's views and ideas for life. Few newspaper articles have had quite this level of impact.

Before delving into reading any text then, it is imperative to ensure students have a good understanding of the conventions, affordances and constraints of its form first. Each component in the 'creating texts' section on page 63 develops this.

What actually is form?

Levine (2016) defines it 'as any arrangement of elements – any ordering, patterning, or shaping'. An experienced writer instinctively knows the conventions, affordances and restraints of form however, these need to be explicitly taught to novices. At secondary level, sometimes we can lean towards an assumption that our students share our own innate appreciation of distinctions in form, which can mean that we do not always explicitly cover these in the classroom and simply jump into the writing or a discussion of what a writer has done with language without consideration of form as well.

Using design and material ideas to consider affordances and constraints

A practical strategy to encourage student understanding here is to give students a list of objects and ask them to identify affordances and constraints for each. For example, wood is durable, but when dry can also provide fuel for fires. Rubber is elastic and can return to its original shape after impact. Clay is malleable, shapeable and reshapable when wet but on firing produces a hard object that retains its shape.

- A rubber ball affords rolling, throwing, kicking
- A sponge affords absorption of liquids
- Wood can be shaped into a chair on which to sit and when placed with other chairs can also encourage social interactions
- Clay affords production of potteryware in all kinds of shapes and designs, for both practical use and artistic merit

All these objects also have some constraints. Rubber deteriorates due to heat and light. Sponges are not useful in building a house. Wooden chairs might be durable but are not particularly comfortable for long periods of time. China is fragile and easily broken once fired. This activity can also be used to demonstrate to children the variation that can come from adapting an item from its original purpose; a chair can be used to stand on and reach an object on a high shelf, functioning as more of a step-ladder; sponges can be used to apply paint in patterns, while slightly more ordinary china plates could be combined into a piece of sculpture.

Form	Affordances	Constraints
Prose fiction	• Large narrative scale over place and time • Significant insight into one or a few key characters • Development of characterisation over time	• Tends to focus on fewer characters (but some writers have been able to circumvent this through multiple points of view)
Poetry	• Conveys intense emotion • Snapshot in time	• Does not develop character or plot over time (except in epics, and not in the same way a novel can)
Drama	• Heightened drama and emotion • Multiple characters	• Typically time constrained in scope • Most of what happens needs to be developed through dialogue alone
Screenplay	• Visual	• Leaves less to the imagination and so, less open to interpretation

Form	Affordances	Constraints
Graphic novel	• Emotion conveyed through images and body language as well as text	• Does not develop emotion or characterisation to the extent that a prose novel does
Journalistic piece	• Clarity • Sharing of information and emotion succinctly	• Short so not possible to develop fully; snapshot overview
Speech	• Immediate • Evocative • Powerful	• Does not necessarily have the same impact not 'in the moment'

Some questions to guide student's consideration of form:

- How is the text laid out on the page? Is there anything distinctive about this, such as headings and sub-headings?
- Does it use all the space on the page or is there a lot of white space?
- Does it have dialogue? Does it have very much writing other than dialogue?
- Are character names written down the side on the left? If so, might it be a play or a screenplay?
- Does it use images?
- How closely are these images linked to the text? Do they form part of the story?
- Does it use lots of flowery descriptive language?
- Is the language used to construct a picture in your head, or is it aiming for clarity in communication?

Obviously meaning is also created through lexis, imagery, grammar, syntax, punctuation, images, and the layout of the page. And so on. Rather than looking at all of these here, the writing and grammar and syntax sections on pages 102 cover some strategies for developing these.

CHAPTER 4
INTERPRETING TEXTS

Reading

Taking our views on curriculum choice from the opening chapter into account, research including the EEF's guide to Improving Literacy in Secondary Schools gives useful evidence-based advice on how to teach reading as part of its recommendations.

It can often feel as though the teaching of all reading in secondary schools is sometimes left to English departments, so this chapter focuses specifically on the teaching of reading in the English classroom as being distinct from whole-school approaches to teaching reading. English as not merely a gateway to other subjects was discussed in the opening chapter.

As such, we must remember the key to disciplinary literacy, which can be defined as the unique uses and implications of literacy within a subject. Essentially, here we are identifying what makes reading as part of English lessons unique. However, what is true of all reading is that once readers are no longer reliant on decoding and can read words with accuracy and speed, then working memory is cleared up to focus on understanding – a key concept that is always useful to bear in mind when considering the teaching of reading.

Reading for pleasure

As an English teacher, it is difficult to detach the concept of reading for pleasure from reading texts chosen for the curriculum. How to encourage and support reading for pleasure is a common question from caregivers. Free choice should be complemented by a well-thought-out curriculum and some of the challenges around recommending books were highlighted in chapter 1 in the 'what even is knowledge' section, and discussed further in the section on 'reading for pleasure' on page 39.

There is probably a balance between recommending books for students and encouraging reluctant readers to read something that they are interested in, but colleagues may find the section on 'form' (page 34) an interesting starting point when trying to recommend books to pupils.

Essentially, we should begin with the fundamental principle that any reading is better than none, and therefore we should avoid making judgements about what students choose to read; there are plenty of anecdotes that indicate that this can lead to young people feeling shame about their choices (World Book Day, 2024). We should come to the discussion with an open mind. This is not to say that to develop our students' reading, we cannot recommend choices that might be more literary and structurally complex with more challenging vocabulary than their choices, but this needs to be in conjunction with validating any reading choice they do make.

For many of us, we read books for pleasure, comfort, assurance, or escape, which we might not want our colleagues to know about if we are trying to maintain an 'intellectual' reading position! There is also the difficulty for secondary teachers that often we are not always totally up to speed with the full depth and breadth of reading materials available to young people in order to make informed decisions. Reading some of those materials so that we can share experiences with our students is important. As Arthur Ransome says, 'any book worth reading by children is also worth reading by grownup persons'. The sheer scope and volume of books published for young people each year presents challenges for the time-constrained teacher here. The Book Trust is a good starting place to see what is available for students of different ages at the moment and, of course, it brings to front and centre the key role of a knowledgeable school librarian.

Defining 'pleasure'

Perhaps a way to help us reconsider how we encourage 'reading for pleasure' is to ensure we are clear on what we mean when we talk about 'pleasure' and importantly where it derives from. Not all things bring pleasure in the same way across time. Pleasure can come from comfort, familiarity, and a sense of revisiting old favourites. This is an entirely natural feeling and one we see typically in toddlers, who keep asking for the same book to be read to them again and again and again. Children, like all human beings, can derive comfort from routine. They like to feel safe, to know what's coming, and to be able to join in.

Pleasure can also come from a sense of adventure and discovery. It can come from a feeling that you are doing something a little bit rebellious and dangerous, such as reading a book that's just a bit too old for you. It can also come from a feeling of having overcome a challenge. *A Clockwork Orange* takes some deciphering, but probably brings a greater sense of accomplishment and achievement in having completed and understood it than say *The Hunger Games*. Both are valid choices. Whilst *A Clockwork Orange* is arguably more canonical and literary, it also requires more diligence, effort and focus to get through. It's a challenge. And we aren't always up for a challenge when we are seeking pleasure because pleasure can also come from feeling like you are doing something well, that it is easy and comfortable and doesn't make you feel stupid. This is of paramount importance to our students who, through their educational journey, are often put in a position of feeling that they do not know anything.

Recently Lucy's daughter (who is in Year 5 at the time of writing) has been reading Alan Garner's *The Weirdstone of Brisingamen* at school. She has loved doing this with her teacher and class, so much so that during half term she wanted to go to Alderley Edge where the novel is set for some literary tourism. She printed maps from the book, planned a route, took a copy of the book with her so when she found a particular stone circle, she could read the description and work out the precise location of the characters in the scene. She loved reading this book however, when she was set the last 80 pages to read on her own at home, she became upset and very demotivated. The book is a challenging text with some quite archaic vocabulary and syntactical construction for a ten year old (who isn't bad at reading) to read independently and she didn't feel confident doing it without the support of her teacher, classmates, and the process of reading it out loud and discussing it.

So let them read *Diary of a Wimpy Kid* because, literary merit or not, there is something about the series that young people identify with. 'Texts are paracanonical if some people have loved and do love them.' Let's just encourage our students to make reading choices that open them up to other kinds of pleasure along with it as well.

Some ways to view (and discuss) pleasure:

- The aesthetics and tactile pleasure of a book as a physical object: what do you like? White crisp pages as yet unturned, or the yellowed stain of ageing and being thumbed by countless hands? The exciting newness of an undiscovered land, or a sense of connectedness to other readers across time?
- Books that bring joy and happiness, through the content, or because of their amusement, entertainment value; books that are playful and fun.

- Books that remind you of love, whether they are about love or because they have a connection to people you love and who have loved you.
- To use consumption as a metaphor, the books we cannot wait for and consume in a single massive gulp, or the ones we nibble at and digest slowly over time.
- Books of assurance and comfort, the ones that remind us of when we were smaller, or happier, that always make us smile when we think of them.
- Books as a mirror to oneself (self-awareness and realisation can bring pleasure)
- Books as a window to the world, encouraging empathy for others.
- Books as a doorway, resulting in a change in consciousness.
- The books that make us aware of beauty.
- Books that show us we belong.

Reading histories

One way in which we can encourage and validate young people's choices is to share our own reading histories and journeys. This is an idea adapted from Dr Alison Waller's book *Rereading Childhood Books: A Poetics.*

What texts have we loved? What did we find hard and struggle with? What is the comfort food of the book world to us? What is the trashy thing we secretly love? How has this developed as we have got older, discovered new tastes, and rediscovered old favourites?

In terms of a practical way to support this, we have found the (free) Padlet timeline to be a useful tool, although other software such as Microsoft Sway could also be used for this purpose. Here is an example: www.padlet.com/lucymcconaghy/reading-journey-9z8znbuhrovb552b. We also set this as an initial mini project for our new intake of Year 7s to discuss with their class teacher, librarian, form tutors, and anyone else in school who engages with students about reading.

Questions to support building reading histories:

- Why did you originally pick up this book/comic as a child? Did you choose it for yourself, was it recommended, or a gift?
- What did you like or dislike, or simply notice, about the cover, about the way it looked?
- Is it yours or did you borrow it from a library?

- When did you read it?
- Where did you read it? How important was place and space in this?
- Who did you read it with? What memories do you have connected with reading this with them?
- What can you remember about the story and characters, the language used, the cover, any illustrations, the smell and feel?
- What were the most important bits of the book/comic for you?
- How did it make you feel?
- How many times have you read it? Why?
- Did it remind you of any other books, or of anything else?
- How do you remember it – through words, illustrations, your own images, stories from parents or friends?
- What did you enjoy about it – did you identify or empathise with characters, love the plot, feel transported to a different world?

Faster Read

Advocates of the Faster Read programme (FR) point to its successes in boosting the reading abilities particularly of struggling readers. We would recommend the University of Sussex's 2019 study (Westbrook et al., 2019) on this as a starting point for anyone looking to delve further into research and evidence. Whilst FR might seem initially somewhat counterintuitive to more traditional approaches to aid understanding in the classroom (reading short sections of text and then spending considerable amounts of time unpicking the construction of the text and in responding), we would observe that English teachers may often show students a film version of a text before reading it to ensure knowledge of plot and character before close detailed study of the text. In our view, FR can accomplish a similar understanding of plot and character, albeit on a slightly longer time frame than a two-hour film, but with a likely greater level of depth and engagement. FR builds whole text understanding, comprehension and inference, and can help with how writers develop character and plot on a whole text scale much more quickly. This is not to say that there is not still a place in the classroom for the unpicking of the text and in written responses however, we would suggest that it builds layers of student understanding to do this once the foundational knowledge of the text has been established. After all, if we had a new text to teach, our own initial response to this would be simply to read the whole text before beginning to annotate it, to choose sections for study, examine its construction, and research contexts.

Questions and methodology for FR

Having trialled FR, we have moved to a balance of whole texts that we initially read in a 'faster read' type way before going back over for closer analysis once students are familiar with the plot and characters. Typically, 60–80% of lesson time is spent reading, with the remaining 20% (or so) on targeted questioning to ensure comprehension, understanding of characterisation, plot, narrative structure and perspectives.

Students need to be clear from the outset that they can put up their hand at any time to ask a question, if they don't understand what has just happened or why a character has acted in a particular way. There is absolutely still time and scope within FR to allow for discussion to develop understanding.

We would also recommend that, especially for FR, texts are read aloud by fluent readers; this might often be the teacher, or another professional colleague in the room. Reading aloud, even when done by a fluent student, does not always help the comprehension of the text that has just been read. Consequently, students' cognitive processes should be allowed to concentrate wholly on the task of understanding rather than being distracted by elements of delivery and prosody, which can instead be modelled by an expert. This could also take the form of audiobook versions.

Reading habits

Like so many elements of school life for our students, reading habits and routines are important to avoid extraneous load when they do read and in order to improve students' reading fluency and accuracy in order to allow them to evaluate texts, and the world around them, critically.

Whichever way reading is approached in English lessons, and dedicated reading lessons may form part of a department's approach to teaching reading as it does for us particularly at Key Stage 3, a consistent approach to expectations around reading is beneficial for students. These could include:

- Expectations around texts being out on the desk, e.g. set texts, dictionaries, support documents, etc.

- Expectations around the sharing of texts, e.g. one text between two people.
- Expectations around annotations.
- Expectations around active reading and listening.
- Expectations around what happens after a text has been read, e.g. answering questions individually or class discussion.
- How, where and when to pack books away.

As Tom Bennett (2020) cites on behaviour, classroom routines can be taught explicitly and so making expectations to students clear around the handling of books and other resources and reading routines is vital in the early stages of working with a class and will also help reduce cognitive load, thereby freeing up working memory for other tasks.

The teaching of reading as part of the English curriculum

Naturally, reading should be central to the planning of a well-sequenced, broad and ambitious English curriculum accessible to all students. Many schools teach English language skills through the study of literary texts and so the purposeful integration of sequential texts and tasks as part of the curriculum is vital. The previous chapter directs us to many of the challenges surrounding text choices, beginning with evaluating what English as a subject is, and so this chapter's focus is on the teaching of reading rather than detailed discussion about *what* students should read. However, it is clear that an effective English curriculum provides the knowledge needed for comprehension and then inference; it ensures that students read often in order to develop fluency; and it includes increasingly challenging texts in terms of vocabulary, syntax, narrative structure and context, chosen and sequenced carefully in order for students to develop those specific areas.

How we read

As an English teacher, it is important that we understand how we read.

Amongst the many resources now available, it may be useful to consider two in particular in order to consider how we read to reflect on the teaching of reading explicitly. Both the 'reading comprehension house' model and the Scarborough's Reading Rope demonstrate to us the complexities of learning to read and the components that require explicit teaching. As a universal offer to all students, if the planned curriculum addresses these key components, then pupils will improve as readers.

There also need to be specific curricular goals matched with the texts that students encounter, added to any cultural capital acquired.

Naturally, there should be whole-school approaches to reading, including the diagnosis of reading ability and interventions required, but this chapter will focus on practical teaching strategies that may be useful for classroom practitioners of English and will merely signpost for colleagues some of the research that informs the rationale behind this practice. Similarly, we will touch upon text choices but, in short, if colleagues are aiming for a challenging yet accessible curriculum for all then careful text choice alongside active reading strategies are imperative.

Rosenshine's (2012) 'principles of instruction' determine immediate strategies that can be implemented in the teaching of reading.

Modelling reading

Pupils need to hear skilled, fluent readers and so English teachers should never be afraid of reading to the class even when options such as students reading aloud may seem tempting in *all* lessons. Much of the teacher-led input discussed in this chapter can develop enthusiasm for students too: fluent reading, excitement about discovering plot or character development, or passion whilst annotating can be infectious for students. Remember what we said about English not being a subject for boys in the first chapter? Here we have a wonderful opportunity to engage all students and encourage enjoyment and interest in English!

Teaching context

An important area to consider when teaching a text – for example the set texts for GCSE English literature – is when to teach the context of the text. If we bear in mind that students need knowledge to make accurate inferences then it can be useful to make curriculum choices about teaching some context before beginning the text. This allows students to have some knowledge (potentially levelling out the pupils' starting points) and keeps them focused on the overall aims of the writer for their implied readers. Once again, approaching context first can be a way to encourage early engagement. Think about the excitement that can be generated by hearing about the Salem witch trials, Windrush, the treatment of the poor during the Victorian period, or the real-life influences on the writer of a dystopian novel.

Recapping prior knowledge

A useful strategy to bear in mind is to think about what knowledge children need in order to understand a text. Rosenshine suggests the review of previous material to build long-term memory and increase fluency of recall. When reading a text with a class, it can be useful to recap students' prior knowledge and encourage students to recall what they have previously learned or read. This can be particularly useful when recalling plot, theme or character development of a full text being studied, or even a short text being used as the vehicle to learn a particular skill, for example for English language. This can take the form of starter tasks on the whiteboard when students enter the classroom, or at points in a lesson, for example through hinge questions as a form of formative assessment before the teacher decides whether to move on to the new material or not. There also always needs to be a place for the 'previously in English' trailer recap by the teacher to ensure that the relevant parts of the previous lesson are recalled.

Mini whiteboard questions, multiple choice tasks, paired discussion and cold calling can be effective methods of allowing the teacher to understand the whole class knowledge of the text before reading or rereading begins and gives the teacher the opportunity to reteach material if required.

Practically, once retrieval materials are created, they can also be shared between colleagues and reused for future teaching or even revision. This can form part of curriculum refinement as mentioned previously. What we also need to bear in mind is that recording evidence does not necessarily mean that students know something – comprehension alone can be purely a form of assessment, and may not always be useful, depending on its context.

Teaching reading: active reading strategies

As the EEF (2021a) states, 'to comprehend complex texts, students need to actively engage with what they are reading and use their existing subject knowledge'. Over lockdown and during remote learning periods, students' subject-specific reading may have been reduced to condensed resources such as PowerPoints. Additionally, it is likely that reading habits of young people will be shifting due to the ever-changing use of technology. Consequently, the type and nature of texts being read will be evolving also. So, it is clear that we will continue to need to build students' resilience in reading for the foreseeable future.

Ensuring active reading works as a form of guide to reading for students. It ensures that they are accountable for what they read and directs them to specific thinking that we want them to experience when they read. The prompts also act as scaffolds to allow students to chunk the information, avoid cognitive overload, and also record quality annotations.

This template can also be easily changed so that the text of any article, piece of literature of wider reading can be copied into the middle column, with little workload for staff in identifying a few relevant questions to scaffold comprehension and deconstruction of the text and its composition.

Reading texts more than once

From the point of view of a passionate teacher, English is naturally a subject that lends itself to rereading texts, but we also benefit from understanding that when we reread a text, we are increasing our reading fluency. Skilled readers who have already read a passage, for example, are able to focus on other components of reading when rereading, such as inference. Rereading a text also helps to avoid cognitive overload whilst also improving students' comprehension.

We must remember that knowledge is needed in order for students to be able to infer: in the model of students knowing more, remembering more and then being able to do more, inferring is the stage that relies on knowledge in order to carry out this process.

When attempting to engage students in rereading texts, we may liken it to them watching a film (or even short clip) for the first time compared to when they watch the film again and are able to notice new things or look for foreshadowing by the director for example. This concept is very much based on Fiorella and Mayer's (2015) select-organize-integrate (SOI) model, where they describe 'a process of making sense, in which you try to understand what is presented by actively seeking relevant pieces of information, mentally organising them, and integrating them with other knowledge you already have'.

Once again, curriculum time dedicated to rereading texts should be created and teachers need to model rereading to demonstrate the value of rereading texts. Home learning can also be utilised for students to complete pre- or post-reading and understanding can be checked via a follow-up activity such as a low-stakes retrieval or knowledge quiz.

If a big idea such as the development of a character or theme is likely to underpin a series of lessons, then it can be useful to reread a passage when you return to it the next lesson. This means that the text needs to be accessible in terms of length to all students. Rereading a text also allows students to undertake rich, meaningful discussions that may not be possible upon first reading, taking into account the SOI model.

One practical strategy with extract work might be:

- Read the passage aloud to the class (modelling).
- Cold call or mini whiteboards to ask about their first impressions about it – this could be in the form of pre-prepared questions.
- Direct students to reread the extract with prompts about what to annotate or make notes on: again, there may be scaffolding provided on a resource to support students. An example might be with George Orwell's *Nineteen Eighty-Four* where second reading may ask students to focus on what dystopian elements Orwell has created or how he uses structure to present the opening setting in a dystopian manner.
- On returning to the extract in the next lesson, it would be worthwhile to reread the passage once more to ensure that the events are brought back into the working memory, enabling students to focus on the next specific component of the big ideas required.

In short, it takes a lot of practice to become a fluent reader: children become better and more confident readers with practice, so opportunity to practise reading needs to be built into the curriculum. Rereading texts allows students to then focus on specific thinking that we want them to experience. The practice of rereading also allows the building of routines and habits for students.

In essence, if we never ask a student to read something without expecting them to do something with it once they have read it, then they will not feel any accountability for what they read. The challenge for teachers, however, is in the planning and scaffolding of these tasks to ensure that no unintentional barriers are created by the tasks associated with the texts read, for example retrieval activities need to be relevant to the thinking that we want our students to undertake, which is why there can be a danger in accessing ready-made retrieval activities online if they do not align with our curriculum intentions.

As suggested by Rosenshine (2012), retrieval practice starters can be provided over time in the form of distributed practice with some schools taking the approach of asking questions from last lesson, last week, last term, last year in order to build schema over time. This can support the comprehension of a text and reading, writing or oracy skills in the form of interleaved practice. Retrieval tasks could include:

- Recalling plot
- 'Who said it?' Key quotation recall
- Grammar starters to recall and practice skills
- Linking of key vocabulary, e.g. satire and misanthropy when studying *A Christmas Carol*

Reading and questioning

As Matt Bromley (2017) notes, 'according to Professor Dylan Wiliam there are only two valid reasons for asking a question in class: either to provide information to the teacher about what to do next, or to cause students to think'.

Opportunities to ask questions planned effectively into the English curriculum are therefore vital. Aimed carefully at particular students, these can both raise confidence as students experience success with reading and recalling or understanding, but also challenge students too. Once again, this is an element of Rosenshine's principles of instruction and needs to be centred around what students have understood from their reading.

- Teachers can plan questions to check student understanding after reading. These can ensure that students are thinking hard about what you want them to think about.
- Use of follow up questions to justify answers: Why has the writer chosen that word in particular? What would the effect be if a different word was chosen? What effect could that have on readers? What could be another way to interpret that?

As always, strategies such as no hands up, providing appropriate waiting (thinking) time and pose, pause, pounce, bounce can be effective.

Text choice as a form of scaffolding

Text choice can also act as a form of scaffolding throughout the curriculum. For example, if Year 9s study a module on dystopian fiction, when they reach Year 10 a familiar passage from Year 9 could be used to avoid extraneous cognitive load and allow them to focus on the skills required for the new key knowledge. We use the opening from *Nineteen*

Eighty-Four in Year 9 as part of a module building knowledge of dystopian literature and its genre conventions, but then return to it in Year 10 when focusing more closely on skills for the language exam.

In this instance, removing the scaffold of text choice could culminate in the Year 10 students working with unseen passages. Increasing the range and variety of texts over time is a curriculum choice where intervention or reteaching may be necessary; a specific text might come to mind that facilitates students accessing specific key knowledge.

Whole class reading books may form part of the curriculum, but reading in lessons for long periods can produce a high cognitive load for all. One useful approach is to reread key sections and include active reading strategies as mentioned previously.

Scaffolding in lessons

Rosenshine (2012) also highlights the benefits of providing students with temporary scaffolds for difficult tasks. For some students, reading itself is a difficult task and so breaking down a longer passage into smaller, more manageable chunks for students can work as an effective form of scaffolding. This could be simply working with a paragraph of a longer text at a time, where one paragraph could be printed at a time, or students could draw a box around a particular paragraph from a longer text that they will focus on.

Checking prompts whilst students read may be a useful form of scaffolding, for example a partly annotated poem that asks questions in order to draw out the intended key knowledge. Check out the two guided reading resources in the appendices for more on this.

Bookmarks that have prompts for students on what they should look for can be useful and form an effective whole department (or even whole school) approach to supporting students' reading. Consider the bookmark resource available in the appendices. We have used these successfully in our school to promote metacognitive strategies for students reading of informational texts, as well as in English.

Other checking prompts may be displaying features of a particular genre alongside a text on a crib sheet, for example gothic, dystopia, persuasive speeches, etc.

Teaching inference

A helpful way to explain inference to students is as a 'judgement of possibilities'. The more of a text we read, the more we know, the more we can make evaluative decisions about whether earlier possibilities are now true or not. For example, give students a single sentence such as 'Tom goes to the gym every morning at 8am', and ask them what they might be able to tell about Tom.

They are likely to offer initial comments such as 'Tom is a creature of habit' and 'Tom wants to be fit', but with pressing they might start to suggest other possibilities: 'Tom picks up a takeaway coffee from the cafe at the gym on his way to work', 'Tom is chatting up someone who works at the gym', 'Tom actually hates working out but his doctor has told him he needs to go to the gym to recover from a heart attack'. Students can then rank these in terms of which of these are more or less probable based on the information given. As a follow up, asking students to reflect on what further information they require in order to make a more accurate inference can help us as teachers focus on their process of evaluation.

Images and inference

Images accompanied by good questioning are an excellent way of getting students to practise their inference skills. Comparison of images is also a good way of supporting students into considering deeper ideas, which can be more challenging initially when those ideas are packaged in 19th century archaic language and syntax, or in the ambiguous richness of verse. Students could be asked to identify similarities and differences between texts (perhaps in a Rally Robin style), and then to summarise these ideas with a single word, which is often likely to lead them towards identifying an abstract concept (more so than text might simply be able to). If images are carefully selected to lead students towards ideas in a text, then this can be a good introduction to subsequently reading that text. For example, two different images of vehicles with the question, 'what can you infer about the owners?', or two different images of houses decorated for Christmas and the question, 'what can you infer about these families?'.

Pre-teaching of vocabulary

Another approach to scaffolding that teachers may find useful in order to optimise intrinsic load is the pre-teaching of key words linked to the curriculum content. This may take the form of students being given Frayer model templates and asked to research the words such as etymology, antonyms, for example, as homework so that they are then able to identify, understand and use the words in future lessons. We have adapted a version of the Frayer model that is used successfully not just in our own English department, but also across the whole school. For example, before students study *A Christmas Carol*, exploring words such as 'redemption', 'Malthus/Malthusian attitude' and 'misanthropic' might be set as homework so that students have the vocabulary to use when approaching the text for the first time. This could also be more closely linked to the context of the novel's publication, if required.

One successful application of this approach is to introduce new vocabulary fortnightly so that students build up their knowledge incrementally over time to help them towards greater success in the accuracy and fluency of independent reading. We take this approach in our department and make sure that students are challenged to use the words over time to ensure that they are not just 'learned' for a test-style performance and then forgotten.

Glossaries of unfamiliar vocabulary can play a part in this strategy, but students should not just be provided with a glossary alone. Alongside providing a glossary, they need to be encouraged to have greater independence in attempting to decode words. They also need to be supported in their reading through explicit vocabulary teaching and the retrieval of these low-frequency words.

Teaching vocabulary: etymology and morphology

One way to provide students with a further strategy to support word decoding is to ask them to understand and consider etymology and morphology. Here is another example where it may feel brave to deviate away from exam technique, but actually we are providing students with the opportunities to decode and build resilience in reading that may prove useful for them in the future, such as understanding propaganda or misinformation, reading between the lines, supporting increasingly academic reading as they progress through their educational journey, or understanding important medical or legal terminology.

Plenty of research has been done on the benefits of explicit vocabulary instruction in the classroom. Less has been done on exactly how this instruction should happen in order to be most effective. Lots of teachers use the Frayer model with varying degrees of success.

The literacy recommendations from the EEF (2021a) point to the importance of decoding the etymology and morphology of words. English is the most wonderful portmanteau of other languages that gives it its unique depth and richness however, this can at times make it difficult for novices to decode. Learning etymology (the origins of words) can help students unravel this varied complexity and make connections between words. It can help with homophonic confusion such as the prefixes 'ante' and 'anti' and so should be taught explicitly as part of vocabulary instruction for those words that have been selected for instruction. Morphology is important because, whilst it does not help with the full meaning (which necessarily stems from the etymological root of words), it can help students make sense of inflexion and help identify word type, verb tense, and so on.

Morphological knowledge is so complex, however, that direct instruction becomes difficult. Professor Kathleen Rastle's work on morphology (et al., 2024) indicates that a good understanding of morphological construction of language is a key component in how adult experts deconstruct and understand meaning (2019). However, the huge morphological variation and diversity of books, as well as the apparent fact that morphology seems to be acquired through wide reading, presents an enormous challenge in the classroom. There is a possible role for explicit morphology instruction, but there is no clear evidence about what should be taught or when, as well as the questions around feasibility (Wood et al., 2024).

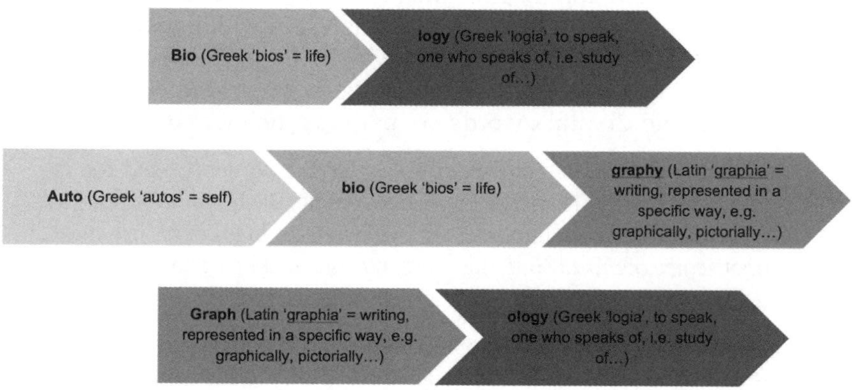

▲ **Figure 1 How etymological knowledge supports new word decoding**

Professor Tim Shanahan (2019) discusses how lexicon works like a network; exploring the connections between words boosts understanding and retention of vocabulary. He also points to the importance of understanding the concept that underpins vocabulary and, therefore, teaching a range of connected words, with synonyms, antonyms, correct and incorrect usage, which can aid understanding and nuance of meaning when the word is used in a text.

As part of her work for the Chartered Teacher Programme, Lucy conducted research that included developing an adaptation of the Frayer model to incorporate both etymology and morphology, and also considering connected words, usage and what the word does not mean, which has subsequently been adopted within our English department and, following some whole staff CPD, in a number of subjects across our school as a unified approach to explicit vocabulary instruction. It is difficult to 'prove' anything through research, but staff appear to like the model as a way of being able to break down the most important words. One of the most significant findings from Lucy's research is the qualitative student voice that indicates students are more likely to use and feel more confident in applying their knowledge of etymology and morphology when it comes to attempting to decode unfamiliar words in a text they read. Lucy's full report is available in the appendices.

Selecting vocabulary to be taught explicitly/learned

Obviously in a language with a lexicon of over 170,000 words, it is not possible to learn all of them. So, English departments and classroom teachers will need to determine which words should be learned (beyond the terminology required to be able to analyse how language and texts are constructed); a more challenging task in English than in some subjects which have words specified to be learned under the national curriculum. David Crystal's words are perhaps the most pertinent here:

> *'Education is the process of preparing us for the big world and the big world has big words. The more big words I know, the better I will survive in it. Because there are hundreds of thousands of big words in English, I cannot learn them all. But this does not mean that I shouldn't try to learn some.'*

For teachers then, it can be helpful to select vocabulary that is relevant to the text being explored, but with potentially wider application. For example, teaching 'Machiavellian' to Year 7 when studying an antagonist such as Long John Silver in *Treasure Island* is an adjective that can equally be applied to many other literary characters. They will need to know that 'buccaneer' is an archaic term to denote a pirate in order to access the text, but its application is much more limited due to a tailing off in usage, as demonstrated by Google Ngram Viewer (a perhaps useful tool in considering which words to teach): https://books.google.com/ngrams/graph?content=bucaneer&year_start=1800&year_end=2019&corpus=en-GB-2019&smoothing=3.

Emotional literacy

We have used our explicit vocabulary instruction as an opportunity to also consider emotional literacy, which in our view has two primary benefits. Firstly, and importantly, it supports students in developing the vocabulary to be able to understand themselves, their own emotions and responses, which has an individual personal development advantage. Secondly, it is often in considering the effects of writers' choices on themselves as a reader that students can struggle to develop or articulate beyond 'it makes me feel sad/bad for such-and-such character'. Interestingly, anecdotal conversations with colleagues in other departments suggests that this challenge in analytical thinking extends to many other arts, humanities and social science subjects and so, considering a Cox whole curriculum perspective suggests that anything that we do to develop students' abilities in English potentially has knock-on improvements across the curriculum.

There are a number of resources online that can support this. For one, we give students Dr Gloria Willcox's (1982) feelings wheel for a range of vocabulary to describe feelings, as well as a word gradient to explore individual words more fully.

In practice, we have attempted to connect explicit vocabulary instruction with our centralised curriculum and to consider our own and likely responses to texts, plots, characters in choosing the emotional literacy words on which we have zoomed in. We are likely to feel frustrated more often than nauseated, so whilst it is a wonderful word, we would choose frustrated for close consideration with students, and then look at an emotion scale/word gradient to determine how it differs from annoyed or irritated.

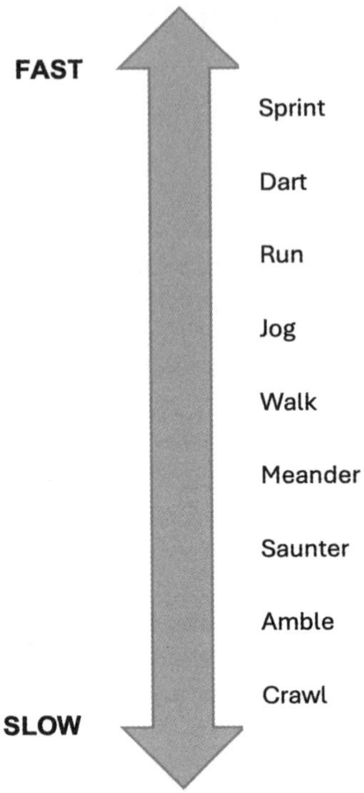

▲ **Figure 2 Word gradient**

Annotating texts

Annotating a text can allow students to create a scaffold for future writing and thinking and the use of visualisers or interactive whiteboards with annotation software allows teachers to verbalise their thought processes as they model annotations for a class.

Many colleagues will find the I-We-You approach to annotating an effective form of scaffolding:

- Teacher models annotations while narrating, particularly when beginning a new text.
- Paired annotations where students support a partner in annotating a section of a text.
- Teacher takes feedback: students add to their own annotations
- Students annotate their texts individually.

This is another example where careful planning can allow confidence and resilience to build over time through spaced practice, and the feedback from annotations can act as a form of formative feedback for the teacher to understand if further input or reteaching is required.

How to model annotating

We see annotating as key to students engaging with a text. So, our approach is to model how to annotate from Year 7. The following table is a guide and an example of the quality of annotations that we would expect, which we include in our 'essential toolkit' that every student receives. The rationale behind this example is that it was produced by a former student to demonstrate that students are capable of this standard.

Like many skills, we model and employ the I-We-You approach to annotating: a Year 7 will receive much more guidance than an Year 11, but whenever we start a new text we will also model and guide with annotations more so that students make a confident start with it.

One of the key challenges once texts are annotated – some students may have beautiful and detailed copies of their texts, decorated with little tabs and post-it notes – is to then guide students to understand how to use them. A key aspect of this transition is then setting a task relevant to their annotations (meaning that you needed to know what to annotate in the first place!) and then the usual modelling and scaffolding to allow students to produce a coherent piece. Once again, it is important to narrate how you are using your annotations in your example in order to show students how their own annotations can act as a vital planning step.

Key advice: Annotating is key to engaging with a text. You will be required to annotate most of the texts you read in English lessons. There are other ways of annotating a text but learn this one to begin with.	
Process	**Explanation**
Underlining/ highlighting	• Read the whole text first underlining or highlighting information or uses of language that seem important to you.
Chunking	• Re-read the text but this time divide it up into manageable 'chunks' that you can explore (the text may already be made up of short paragraphs that can serve as chunks but there may also be longer paragraphs which need to chunked). • Give each chunk a title which sums up the key idea described in the chunk, e.g. 'setting' 'relationship – father/daughter'. • Write a question next to each chunk, e.g. Why has the writer mentioned this?/Why is the writer spending so much time on describing the setting? • Write something else that you have understood, e.g. The father seems to have a grudge against his daughter/the weather is unnaturally cold. • Underline key uses of language, e.g. The father eyed her coldly. • Analyse more closely – zoom in on language and ideas, e.g. 'coldly' – adverb – he is hostile towards her, not warm or paternal. • Now consider what the writer's overall purpose may be, e.g. To explore the impact of the setting on relationships/to explore tensions within families.
Group annotation	• Finally… cover your page with annotations as you discuss the text in your class/group discussions!

You'll find an annotated version of Percy Bysshe Shelley's Ozymandias in the appendices.

Summarising

At times, it may be appropriate for teachers to summarise a text before reading it through with a class. Similarly, an activity such as summarising what students have just read ensures that students think hard as they are forced to consider the most important aspects of what they have read: this has been proven to have been a success by Fiorella and Mayer as a generative learning approach and is demonstrated effectively by Enser and Enser (2020).

Similarly, rich interactions around a text such as structured discussion questions are also valuable. If reading electronic texts, students could still be asked to summarise and also be asked to find supporting evidence to ensure they are fully engaging with the content of the text.

Students reading aloud

While we have already drawn attention to the need for teachers to model reading to students, it is also important to listen to students read. Listening to pupils read allows teachers to understand not only what the pupil's internal voice might sound like but also their fluency and automaticity. It gives teachers a chance to feedback to the student on any of these areas.

This approach can be implemented when pupils read individually with the teacher whilst the rest of the class carry out independent work. We do this particularly at Key Stage 3. Teaching assistants could also support with listening to students read or supporting other students whilst the teacher listens to readers. This method also circumnavigates the unwillingness of some students to read to the rest of the class, although there are other options such as choral reading or echo reading, for example, which insists on full class participation.

When reading aloud, teachers should actively encourage students to control their prosody to further encourage oracy as a core concept of English lessons. This is where curriculum text choice also comes to the fore, for example reading poetry and drama aloud. Again, it can also be an excellent opportunity to praise those students who may often be quieter or those students who are excellent verbally but struggle when writing.

Reading lessons

Reading lessons may form part of an English curriculum and it is important to remember that pupils who are reluctant readers or are struggling to read often require scaffolding and support. These aspects must be considered when planning silent reading lessons.

First of all, book choice may be random by poor readers and so some guidance is required for these students. This may be the role of a school librarian, it may be guided through book banding from a reading programme, or English teachers may need to have discussions with their students about what they read, and listening to readers as suggested above may allow these conversations to provide more fruitful guidance to students.

Challenges around book recommendations by English teachers can include:

- English teachers have not read everything!
- Do teachers read young people's fiction?
- How can you 'sell' the classics?
- Should students focus on reading fiction or non-fiction?
- Are electronic texts as valuable as print texts?

So, teachers need to be prepared for these conversations, which can equally happen at the request of supportive caregivers at parents' evenings too.

When planning reading lessons, there need to be specific links between texts chosen and specific curricular goals. In our setting, we could take a Year 9 group as an example, where each class is allocated one reading lesson per fortnight, led by an English teacher. Curricular goals are linked to the specific sequence of learning as part of the overall English curriculum and so, in the reading lesson, students will experience specific taught areas such as inference and skimming and scanning with age-appropriate texts. Students then apply these skills independently in their chosen reading books to practise these skills further whilst the teacher takes it in turn to listen to one student at a time read to them. Check out the reading lesson resource in the appendices.

Print or screen?

At our school, all staff have been required to produce careers profiles to share with students our own careers journeys. One aspect of this has included the question, 'What recent innovation or development in your field has amazed you?' Lucy's response to this was initially perhaps somewhat flippant as the question felt geared more towards STEM subjects, but does in fact point to some truth about the significance of the printed word:

> *'For me, it is the invention of the printing press (ok, not really recent – Gutenberg's invention was around 1440!) – but it revolutionised knowledge itself, making it accessible easily and cheaply to everyone. All of the learning and development that has happened since, in every field, in every subject in school, in literacy, even in the existence of universal education itself, stems from the printing press.'*

Perhaps there is even more significance than merely the development of all knowledge and learning for the human race in the last 600 years. More recent technological innovations and advancements, which have enabled even greater sharing of information and the written word mean that a not insignificant amount of reading nowadays takes place on an electronic screen rather than the page of a printed book. A hugely pertinent question for teachers of English to be asking therefore is what is the impact of this? Are all forms of reading, in whatever guise, through whatever media, equal? Whilst it is not yet possible to answer this question comprehensively, the indicators currently appear to be pointing pretty unequivocally to a resounding 'no'.

Delgado et al's 2018 study 'yield a clear picture of screen inferiority, with lower reading comprehension outcomes for digital texts compared to printed texts', as well as pointing to differences between reading on a computer screen and on a handheld device, as well as whether the reading involves scrolling (which tends to detract from reader engagement with the text).

This is further substantiated by the neurophysical aspects of digital versus print reading investigated by Frouda et al (2023). Causes of screen inferiority for reading are not yet fully understood, but perhaps a factor in reading digitally rather than in print is the additional skills involved in accessing the mode: the digital literacy skills that are required to be able to navigate a text, and typically involve more multi-tasking and therefore greater cognitive load, compared with simply holding a book and turning a page. The (technologically enabled) ability of students to simply copy information online rather than properly engaging with it in terms of understanding also means that we need to be careful about any reading we ask students to do electronically. It should always be accompanied by questions or tasks that ensure engagement and build comprehension.

We would also like to make it clear that we are absolutely not against innovation in the classroom, or against technology per se. We use loads. It's about applying the appropriate tool for any task.

In conclusion, while there has been no wholesale comprehensive study on reading abilities and the relationship with reading on screens or on the page, the smaller scale and anecdotal evidence point to the superiority of reading printed word rather than digitised in improving reading skills. And tying this to the decline in reading over the last decade, it might be possible to draw a conclusion (entirely unsubstantiated, we accept, but further research absolutely needs to be undertaken in this area) that reduction in levels of reading might not only correlate with reduced time in school, and therefore direct input is required from experts trained in developing reading skills to counter the effects of the covid-19 pandemic, but also a likely increase in screen use during that time, including reading more texts electronically. There is a caveat however as we also see the benefits of engaging digital reading: firstly where it benefits those students with SEN and can be used to support their learning; secondly in terms of technology as a tool to make access to texts easier; and thirdly in terms of student engagement and opt-in.

If we can get reluctant readers to engage with text on a screen but not in printed version, then at least they are reading something and in some capacity. Doing anything is better than doing nothing. But if we want to do it well, then the evidence seems to be leading towards continuing with the printed word. Long live books!

CHAPTER 5
CREATING TEXTS

The teaching of writing in secondary schools, as the opening chapter began to touch on, perhaps needs to be the main focus currently for questions about the 'what', 'how' and 'why' in English. Much has been done on curriculum design and reading, but less so to improve students' experience of writing in schools. Teachers, with the best intentions of developing students' critical responses to literature at GCSE, can focus on critical analytical writing as the standard response to many texts students read (whether structures to support and scaffold this are PEE, PRETZL, WHW or other). This is understandable in a time-constrained curriculum and with a workforce who are predominantly literature (and therefore reading) specialists.

English teachers are often not writers; they are more likely to be literary critics than anything else. However, when considering writing, we need to think about *what* students are likely to be asked to write in the English classroom. In an ideal world, they would both encounter and be able to master writing in the widest possible range of forms, for different audiences and purposes. In reality, in a time-constricted curriculum preparing students for the narrow confines of GCSE English literature and language, the likelihood is that they will be asked to write critically (theoretically building towards a literature essay, although rarely practised as a whole entity), or for the relatively narrow typical tasks and purposes of GCSE language, for example, the opening of a story or a description of an image, a letter, a newspaper article for a broadsheet newspaper, an essay, speech, or the nebulous 'text for a website'.

Yet if you were to ask an English expert to list all the possible forms of written communication, there are so many missing from this list: play scripts; film and TV scripts; the typical communication of web forums and social media; travel guides; recipe books; memoir, biography and autobiography; journals and diaries; graphic novels and comics; poetry in its many, many forms and guises; fan fiction; podcasts; marketing and PR communications; editorial work; advertising, to name a few.

Many of these can be studied at A-level in English language and literature or A-level English language, and definitely at university level study, but the narrow focus and range of tasks at Key Stage 4 and often subsequently in Key Stage 3 to 'prepare' for Key Stage 4 means most students don't even realise that studying these forms of writing, or creating them themselves, is even an option.

The sheer variety of these forms of communication seems overwhelming when we begin to consider how to incorporate those into the curriculum. In our view, it seems sensible to expose students to possibility in Key Stage 3 (bearing in mind they may have encountered a reasonable range of these already at primary school or outside of a school setting) to realise the potential ahead if they continue to study English, and then to hone and perfect a narrower range at GCSE.

Alongside the dual challenges of a narrow GCSE assessment framework and competing time pressures is the predominance of written response type to any text that students ever read: the critical essay (or paragraph at least). While we consider how to curate a reading curriculum that encapsulates cultural literacy and also diversity, whilst stimulating and challenging students, we also need to consider how we do, should and could ask them to respond to those texts. In the English classroom this is often in the form of academic critical analysis; the argument being this forms the majority of assessment in both English language reading and all of GCSE literature.

We are not refuting the importance of teaching essay writing for a second. However, if every time students read a text, no matter how exciting, how carefully chosen that text is, they are always asked to respond with exactly the same form of written text, with the same structure and conventions, we can see how the subject can quickly become dry and boring despite teachers' best efforts in curriculum design. Therefore the nature and variety of written responses needs to match the variety of reading material students are exposed to, as well as according each status and merit. As Webb (2020) says, 'Writing is art. All writing.'

Teaching form in writing

Students in secondary school have already been exposed to a range of forms of writing both at primary level and through their own reading, however some of their knowledge of the conventions and characteristics of these may be implicit. Even the term 'form' is not always explicitly taught in the classroom.

The following activity is a good way of making thinking about this visible and explicit (Webb,, 2020):

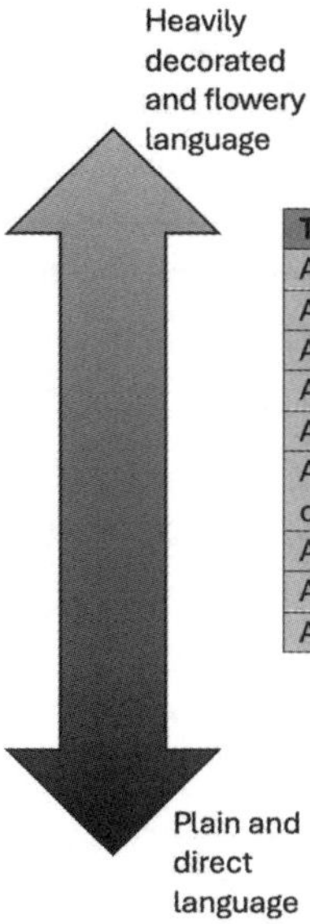

Types of writing
An informative newspaper article about a road traffic accident
A short sort about a child getting lost in a supermarket
A set of instructions for how to put together a flat-pack bookcase
A speech arguing that nurses should be paid more money for the work they do
A letter to persuade an employer to give you a summer job
A newspaper article arguing that smoking is a disgusting cancer at the heart of our society and must be eradicated
A poem about a sunrise
A monologue spoken by a character following the death of a loved one
An essay exploring misogyny in Thomas Hardy novels

Order these types of writing according to how you think they are likely to use language: plain or flowery?

▲ **Figure 3 Types of writing activitity**

Using questioning to draw out reasoning and judgements that students make – and in comparison to each other – around formality and 'literariness' of these texts will draw out what students already know about language choices in written texts. Then, discussing the characteristics and conventions of these in more detail, often with checklists as a useful metacognitive tool for students to apply themselves, can help in the classroom with discussions of form.

Start me up

One area students can often struggle with when writing is actually getting started. We firstly need to acknowledge that there are two separate (although connected) challenges when it comes to students writing articulately and fluently. The easier one of these to support in the classroom is in expressing ideas whilst a more significant challenge is in 'having ideas' in the first place. The work of Friedlander (1990), Miller et al (2012) and Tan et al (2019) all point to socioeconomic factors as well as the significance of EAL in building students' cultural capital to a level where they might have a view on any given topic in order to have something to write about. This is much harder to teach. And this applies to all students within our classrooms: we have all also experienced the student who sits there and says 'I don't know what to write' when asked to get started. Actually having ideas can sometimes be a bigger barrier than vocabulary or being able to craft a metaphor.

The following ideas are all ways of overcoming the blank page's unbearable weight of massive expectation when it comes to constructing narratives across a range of forms of writing.

Ice breakers to stimulate creativity and overcome fear of white space can help, such as:

- Image prompts: we have found the Literacy Shed website to have some unusual images that often provoke ideas amongst students.
- Character scenarios (see the next section).
- Starting part way down the page and a little way into a story.
- First lines and sentence starters: some great resources available from:

  https://storywritingacademy.com/one-sentence-writing-prompts/ and

  https://www.literacyshed.com/the-story-starter-shed.html.
- The dot: this is a method by Sai Murray that is originally suggested in *Teach Like a Writer* (Webb, 2020). The method involves using plain rather than lined paper to overcome ideas about writing having 'rules', and then simply drawing a (bold and unapologetic) dot or squiggle on it. Then one piece can be chosen and discussed as if it were a piece to hang in an art gallery. The point of this activity is to demonstrate to students that all audiences bring their own interpretation to someone else's work whether that meaning was intended or not. This can also be a good way to introduce students to reader-response theory and to promote debate about the extent to which meaning is created by writers or by readers.
- Use mini-whiteboards: for some students, the anxiety over beginning and 'getting it wrong' can prevent beginning at all. The flexibility of a whiteboard, of knowing they can easily edit, rub out, start again if they so wish can sometimes motivate students to make a start, any start. To modify Steinbeck, 'And now that you don't have to be perfect', you can begin.
- Paired work: this can take the pressure off individual students feeling they need to produce some kind of output; allow an initial

collaboration and exchange of ideas that gives all students some kind of material to then work with.

- Write on something unusual: sugar paper, tissue paper, even with chalk pens on the classroom windows! This can sometimes break a creative barrier.

Creating character, scenario and plot

Some of these ideas are adapted from Jacob Ross and Zodwa Nyoni in *Teach Like a Writer* (Webb, 2020).

- Generating ideas through images – print images of people, or collect them from magazines (civilians, not celebrities).
- Give students two of these at random and then consider how they could connect these people together.
- What motivates them?
- Give a location where both characters are. Include a level of challenge or variation that takes them beyond the scope of their own lives
- Now, the complication – there is a secret that exists between them. How is this shared?

Time

Place your character on a temporal spectrum:

- Something has happened to them in the past which has consequences for them in the present.
- Something is happening to them right now (or perhaps a lack of anything happening could be the pivotal idea).
- Something is about to happen to them in the near future that will have consequences for the character.

Locations

- Inside a fridge.
- In a mosque/church/synagogue/temple.
- Stuck up a tree that is on fire.

Secrets and complications

- One of your characters has killed someone.
- Your character woke up this morning on a train and doesn't know how they got there.

- One of your characters is slowly turning invisible.
- One of your characters is missing their brother's wedding today.
- Someone accuses your character of a crime they have not committed.

Questions

- What's in their pocket?
- How did they get the papers that are in their jacket?
- Why are they missing mass this evening?
- What did someone do that they are covering up?

Write like a prose fiction writer

As character and narrative are key components in prose fiction (of whatever length), the ideas above are all useful in beginning to write prose.

Create a character profile. This should be someone who could be dropped in anywhere. Middle-aged working parents can be found in all sorts of locations – in a yurt or market, on a train about to be hit by an enormous wave, at the 'Where's Wally' zoo (AQA Paper 1 2023), whereas it is going to take some explaining as to how your medieval knight has ended up there. Students can then use their character in a range of different situations; this is a 'here's one I made earlier' approach that can support students for creative writing at GCSE but still ensure creativity and a direct response to specific prompts.

Character questions:

- Basic information: name, gender, age
- Where are they from? (although perhaps avoid dialect choices that might be difficult to maintain consistently)
- Family
- Job or previous occupations
- Religion/faith

To generate a plot, with the building blocks of narrative, this character then needs to have the following introduced:

- Initial situation
- Danger
- Resolution (or absence thereof)

Images

Teachers could use a particular painting or image for this. The Literacy Shed offer a few that we have found work consistently. Often contrasts and objects in unusual settings work well as stimuli, such as as a soldier playing a piano in a forest, or a house full of sand, a child pegged to a washing line, or buildings in unusual places.

Write like a screenwriter/playwright

We have included these together as there are some synergies in the purpose and nature of these two forms that merit being considered together; namely the focus on action and dialogue as opposed perhaps to lengthy descriptive writing, together with a heightened sense of dramatic tension.

To really understand drama, students need to not only read plays but also, crucially, they need to watch them. We know it's a massive faff to organise a trip or even to have a travelling theatre company visit whose performances are specifically designed for school settings, but it is worth it, and for many students this is the only drama they will experience.

Promoting drama

We as English teachers have a role to play in promoting drama in the classroom. Why write a play when so many people watch tv and film? Why go to see one? And we need to point our students to the visceral, living nature of drama, the living breathing immediacy of it, the concepts of melodrama and catharsis, the fundamental elements of collaboration, construction and interpretation, which all enhance meaning in dramatic texts, as opposed to the somewhat more fixed elements and slow build of a novel. They work in different ways and are trying to achieve different things.

Stimuli for creating drama

Fundamentally these and the supporting questions that teachers ask need to centre around human emotion, as well as steering away from cliché.

Images are often good prompts for creating drama, looking at a still scene from a photograph or painting. Students could be asked to create a still image, and then develop this further by considering what happens to the narrative (or characters) if the angle were different, or the camera moved two metres to the left? What changes?

This can then be developed through thought tracking to build up characterisation.

- What sort of character – the protagonist, supporting, minor?
- Ask students to create and flesh out a back story for their character.
- Character is predominantly revealed through dialogue and action – what they do and say predominates, unlike in prose.

In the manner of...

A great drama activity for getting students to consider how to convey characterisation and emotion without being able to describe it is this game. Give students a verb (e.g. 'walk'), and then ask them to come up with their own adverb which will show how their character is carrying out this action. Other students can try to guess to see if they are correct.

Poetry can also be good as a prompt for drama, sharing as the two forms do a sense of heightened emotion, as well as thinking about scenarios which could increase drama, such as fragmented memories (for example due to a brain injury or dementia): what would come out? What would the impact be?

Screenplays

Many of these ideas also work for writing screenplays; students however also need to be taught some additional terminology and conventions in terms of the layout of the form. Looking at some examples of printed scripts alongside watching a film/tv version will also show students the idea that the script is a living, breathing thing that is often slightly different to the final polished performance that they see recorded. Texts could be chosen for this that run thematically alongside the rest of the curriculum: for example we use scripts from *Wednesday* as part of our Gothic unit, as the previously-acquired knowledge of the Gothic genre allows students to focus their attention more on the construction of the text.

It is worth showing your students a layout of a screenplay, which is easily found via a Google Image search.

Write like a poet

This is often an area where students are expected to read and comment (as analysing poetry forms a substantial part of GCSE and A-level study of English Literature), but are less frequently asked to create a poem themselves. Perhaps though, poetry is the one form we should be encouraging them to write above all others. Poetry dwells 'in possibility' (Emily Dickinson); it is 'thoughts that breathe and words that burn' (Thomas Gray), and it 'begins in delight and ends in wisdom' (Robert Frost). What could be more important?

In any attempt by English teachers to overcome the challenges of socio-economic background and cultural capital, Audre Lorde's (1984) words about poetry as a social equaliser are of huge significance: 'Of all the art forms, poetry is the most economical. It is the one which is the most secret, which requires the least physical labor, the least material, and the one which can be done between shifts, in the hospital pantry, on the subway, and on scraps of surplus paper... poetry has been the major voice of poor, working class, and Colored [sic] women. A room of one's own may be a necessity for writing prose, but so are reams of paper, a typewriter, and plenty of time.'

Getting started: what is a poem?

Look at 'what poetry is' in the classroom. We particularly like the William Carlos Williams poem *This is Just to Say* for discussion as it always provokes thoughtful debate: is it a poem or simply the kind of note you might leave on a fridge? What makes it poetic? Why has it been arranged the way it has on lines? Is this what makes it poetic?

This poem also presents opportunities to talk about prosody when it comes to poetry and its performative element. Someone reading this poem reads it aloud differently to the way they would if it were presented as prose – the pace is slower, each word is lingered over and savoured, just like the plums. In poetry, meaning can be created by white space, by pauses. To demonstrate this, you could take a mundane item of prose, such as a receipt, a staff memo, or a shopping list, and look at poetic placement. How does incorporating line breaks emphasise certain words by placing them at the beginning or end of a line? And then there's punctuation. Once you have broken up a text with lines, punctuation can become less necessary than in prose, so its use or not is more of a conscious choice by the writer.

Song lyrics are also useful. You could give students a range of songs and poems, perhaps without titles and authors, and ask them to sort them into which ones are poems and which are songs. Rap can often work well here because of the frequent use of sound effects such as assonant rhyme.

There is an irony that as literary forms go, poetry has more options, more constraints, more rules than any other; yet also has more freedom, more variety, more capacity to break the rules at the same time. Once students have got over an idea of poetry being a particular thing and have seen it in many shapes and guises (and debated whether some of this even is poetry), they may feel more confident about writing their own.

Key Stage 3

Some favourite resources to get students writing, particularly at Key Stage 3, include the following:

Kit Wright's *The Magic Box*

Key questions to accompany this:

- What can you put in a box?
- What can't you put in a box?
- Why would you put it in a box?
- What would a box like this be like?
- What could you do with the box?

Dean Atta's *I Come From*

Key questions to accompany this:

- Where do they come from?
- What reminds them of home, of family?
- What values and ideas are important to shaping who they are?

The next poem I write will ...

This one is a little meta and takes away some of the pressure to produce something now, acknowledging and allowing the poem to not be 'perfect'. Students can identify any aspects of writing they are struggling with and incorporate these into their poem, for example 'the next poem I write will rhyme', when this one does not. It's a good way of exploring what a poem can and should be and whether they have to follow the 'rules'. Get students to identify things they struggle with when asked to write a poem (or anything creative!). They can then incorporate these into their poem. These provide relatively scaffolded frames for students to begin and to feel they have a structure for their poem, whilst still allowing plenty of scope for creativity and their own individual voice and experiences.

The best words in the best order

Coleridge was right. Poetry is the most economical form of writing, the most powerful, the most compact; and so every word counts, more. Editing and redrafting to find the best words is then even more paramount when writing poetry. Every single piece of punctuation or its absence, every word, every placement of every word, every last little detail conveys meaning. See the section on page 98 on editing.

Poets and their drafts

Some earlier drafts of poems can be found online, for example in the British Library online archive (such as Owen's *Dulce et Decorum Est* or Blake's *London*), which can be used to highlight to students that even famous poets edit their work and the significance of their choices in redrafting. A book, *Poems in Progress* (2022) which compiles and discusses many such poems is also available (it's a delight) and includes work by practising poets as well as drafts in a range of languages in addition to English; it includes drafts by Owen, Plath, Armitage, Blake, Angelou, Zephaniah, Kipling to name a few – many writers who are likely to feature in the English classroom.

Authentic voice

Expose students to writers who incorporate their authentic voice, dialect, accent, even speech impediment, into their writing. This might often include performances by those poets, so listen to Seamus Heaney reading his own work, or Philip Larkin, Tony Harrison, Pam Ayres, John Agard, Patience Agbabi, Amanda Gorman.

Get a poet in

There are a few contemporary poets who work with schools. Our own experiences of this have been really enriching for our students and have encouraged an appreciation for and love of poetry, as well as the performance of poetry. It is especially lovely to see the kind of students who don't always have lots of experience of achieving success in a school setting being creative and getting recognition for their work.

Performance

We organise an annual poetry recital where students, staff and friends of the school come together to read poems they have written or love. It takes an English department to bring this together, with all teachers promoting it with students and encouraging participation, as well as across school. A really important aspect for us is the buy-in and support from our colleagues in other departments – it makes a huge difference to students to see one of the receptionists, the head's PA, their favourite science teacher, all sharing their love of poetry, especially when they stand up and recite Byron completely from memory or a grime mix of Chaucer!

Poetry on the internet

Modern technology has its advantages as well as its issues. If poetry is the great equaliser, then the internet is the means through which it has become accessible, the mode necessarily supporting poetry's unique spoken form. The internet has given us the work of poets such as Testament, for example, whom we use alongside study of William Blake as Testament talks freely of his admiration of Blake and has a wonderful hip-hop influenced version of *London (remixed)*. It also allows us Instapoetry and YouTube poets: the Rupi Kaurs, Chloë Fraynes and Atish Chintalwars of the world. Encourage students to go out there and find them on Instagram, TikTok, or whatever platform comes next. Just like *Diary of a Wimpy Kid*, it's variable in its literary merits, but then there's equally no consensus on the quality or merits of D. H. Lawrence's finest poetic works either.

Write (and illustrate) like a graphic novelist

If we are serious about reclaiming what English should encompass in the secondary classroom, then that needs to include reading and writing in all forms and avoiding snobbery about certain sorts of texts, focusing instead on how to teach them as writing forms and through academic study in their own right.

Those 'reluctant readers' of classic novels might turn out to be avid enthusiasts of graphic novels but don't perceive the reading that they do here to actually be reading, because no one has ever told them it counts and they have never had the opportunity to study it in a classroom, except perhaps as a 'storyboard the plot events' type of cover lesson we have all set out of necessity from time to time.

We would also add a note that graphic novelisation of challenging texts can also be a useful tool for allowing students to access those texts initially and can be particularly useful for certain SEND students – many of the GCSE literature texts have these in teacher and student revision guides.

Graphic novels in our curriculum

We incorporated a graphic novel as part of a unit looking at dystopia and used (due to its use of expletives, a very carefully selected) extracts from one of the *Snowpiercer* graphic novels. It is worth noting that this unit also included extracts from scripts for *The Last of Us* to allow students to consider and develop their understanding of dystopian conventions within other forms of media as well, including computer games with extensive narrative structures and characterisation, and TV drama.

Terminology

Introduce students to concepts first. Images (perhaps unsurprisingly given the form) are particularly useful for this, so for example rather than teaching students the term 'mise-en-scene', give them a page that incorporates image and text, and then get them to answer the simple question 'what did you focus on first?' Drawing out discussion about why a particular feature captured their attention and then any differences with other students introduces this key concept in understanding how graphic novels and comics convey meaning, which is structurally different to many other texts students encounter where the writer rather than the reader is in complete control of the reader's sequencing of the text.

Drawing attention to the process of reading a graphic novel, with intentionality, will help to develop students' awareness of how they read a text and how this particular form differs from other forms. This then begins to scaffold students' ability to analyse this kind of text.

We then introduce some new vocabulary. The following example from *Orwell's Animal Farm: The Graphic Edition with CSEC Study Guide* is a good one because it covers some key aspects of graphic novels for Key Stage 3 students without overwhelming with the full detail students would need to be able to analyse the form at a higher level of study. We found that students were largely familiar with the ideas underpinning terminology anyway, so all we were doing was forefronting them and giving the students an academic language in which to express their ideas. We then asked them to apply these to an example of a graphic novel and to discuss how the form was able to convey its dystopian ideas and tropes, considering the interplay between text and images, as well as focusing on the very sparse and carefully chosen words. In creating their own texts, it is really important with graphic novels to dedicate time to careful editing; the smaller amount of words used means that each must necessarily be carefully chosen.

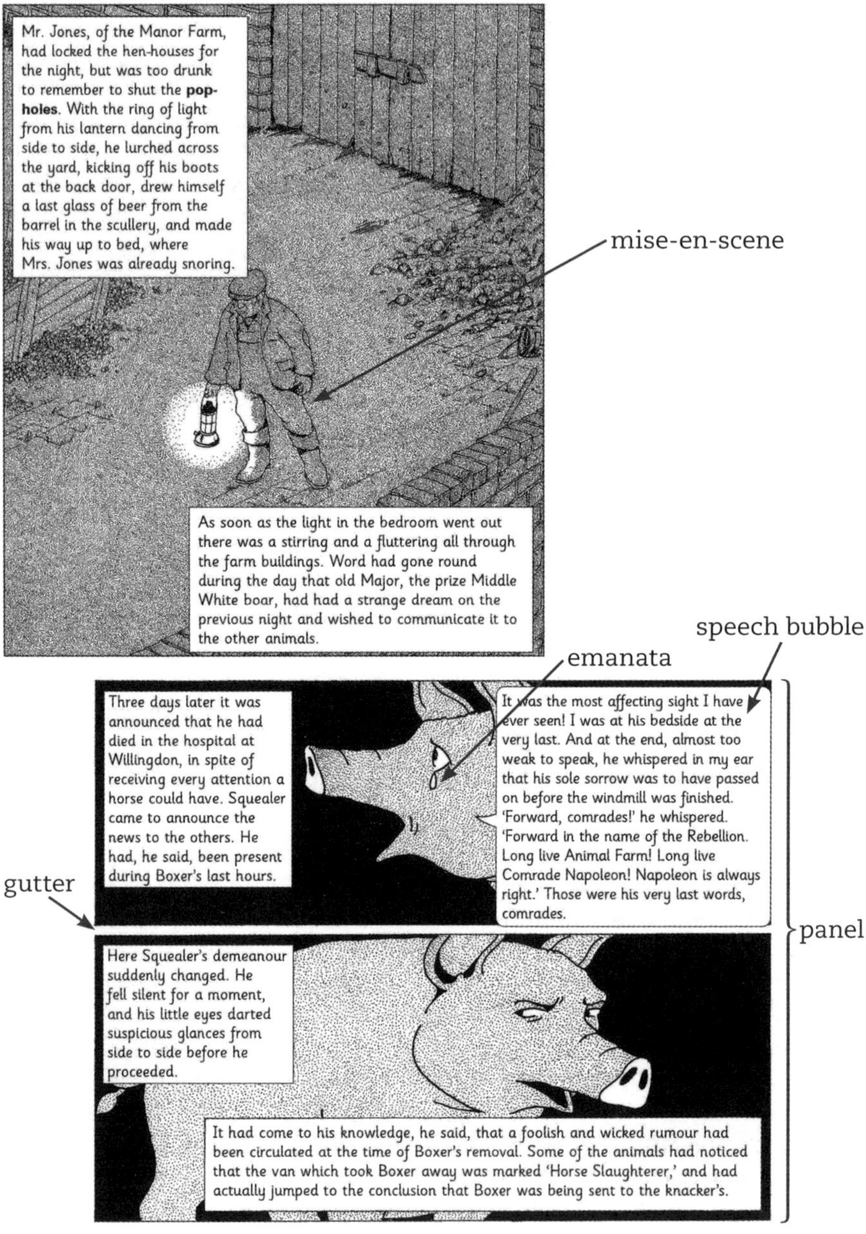

▲ **Figures 4 & 5 Comic strip from Orwell's Animal Farm: The Graphic Edition with CSEC Study Guide**

Write like a journalist

Journalistic writing is potentially something students might be asked to do within a GCSE English language exam, or to read articles taken from newspapers. And even if not, the primary objective of journalistic method is to obtain truth and present it with clarity – critical evaluation skills indispensable for young people navigating the modern world and all its forms of communication.

In our view, students are often unaware of the nuances of journalistic writing. There is often a perception that all journalistic writing is to produce factual news reports, but paradoxically that all journalism is also skewed and biased. Unpicking the thinking behind these misconceptions can be challenging; a way to counter it effectively in the classroom though is to explicitly teach about journalistic **method** and **process**.

This needs to include a real-world journalistic style writing task – one which is relevant to the context of our students and achievable.

Purpose

Students could be asked to determine what the primary purpose of journalism (or in fact a range of different written forms is). They need to have a clear understanding that the purpose of literature (fiction, poetry, drama), is to entertain, amuse, and to make people feel or imagine something. Literature is primarily concerned with the *beauty* of the written word, while truth is the primary purpose of journalism, and subsequently the most important thing is the *clarity* of writing.

Types of journalistic writing

A bullet point list comparing differences between news reporting and feature writing could be a useful checklist tool for students to refer to and be directed to for metacognition.

Students could also be given the features of each type of writing and asked to sort them into the two categories. When set any writing task, they need to be absolutely clear on which form of journalism they are being asked to undertake. At GCSE it will be more of a feature piece than news reporting, which in itself can cause problems when students' perception is that journalism is primarily concerned with news reporting.

Types of journalistic writing	
News/reporting	**Features (opinion pieces, editorials, etc.)**
• Precision, accuracy, unbiased • Typically uses inverted pyramid structure – all important details need to be at the start – front loaded, in case anything is edited out • Must keep your reader in mind – what do they know or need explaining?	• Scope for opinion and humour • Different structure: begin with a killer quote, or a 'drop intro' (delays the subject for engagement) • Then followed by a 'nutgraf' – a nutshell paragraph which points out why this story matters and the context • Followed by some background and then the main body, which should flow like a narrative • Carefully crafted conclusion at the end (different to a new articles where the most important information is at the start)

The structure of a feature piece is detailed above. Students could also look at the inverted pyramid model of a news report, which will help with an understanding of editing and why the piece is structured this way.

▲ **Figure 6 Inverted pyramid model of a news report**

The journalistic method/process

Introduce students to how a real-world journalist operates; facilitate a class discussion about how journalist method and process allow journalists to achieve their primary objective of truthful clarity (except for crafting, which we will come to shortly).

Journalistic method
• Brainstorming: what do you already know about this topic? Identify what you don't know but need to find out
• Research data
• Interviews: range of accounts from different sources
• Fact-checking
• Crafting, cutting, editing (length and focus requirements)

Editing

It is rare for a journalist to be asked to produce a piece without any constraints so, any task should contain a word limit that you must strictly enforce!

As part of their real world piece, students should be encouraged to redraft and edit, both for clarity and concision. This may be best modelled by the teacher, for example using pre-prepared examples or live modelling under a visualiser (or similar technology).

Students could then be given an additional challenge, to edit down their original piece due to editorial constraints, where they are then required to cut out parts of their writing. This is most likely to be effective and valuable as part of a class discussion about the challenges of this, and why they made certain decisions to edit and cut. What effect did this have on the overall piece?

Before moving to doing this in their own work, they could be given a text on which to practise for example, Jamie Oliver's parma ham, figs and mozzarella salad recipe is one we like to use in the classroom. However, if looking to use another example of your own, it's important to choose one that includes a number of adjectives and adverbs to make the editing exercise meaningful.

Exposure to feature pieces: we are what we read/consume

Undoubtedly, the more we read of a genre or form of writing, the more we begin to understand its nuances; familiarity embeds understanding. So, we need to intentionally expose our students frequently to forms of writing they do not necessarily choose to read regularly for themselves. For many this includes newspaper feature and opinion pieces. We recommend the 'guided reading' section on page 80 for suggestions for a way this could be accomplished.

Write like a (good) blogger

One of the – at times, wonderful – affordances of the advancement of social media and the internet is the equity in its levelling of the publishing playing field. Anyone can become a writer and can publish their work online – with varying degrees of success and quality – and so, much more work, research, innovative ideas and resources are being shared online. Much of the teaching community has benefited from this.

If our students become writers, the likelihood is that this is more likely to be online. They can also be asked to write text for a blog as part of English language GCSE. So, let's teach the conventions, affordances and constraints of blogs. Maybe we could even get our students to create, produce, develop, edit and run with their own blog.

Conventions

- First person, personal opinion and experience
- Typically related by subject matter in topic and post: blogs can be journalistic, offer commentary and critique, academic or reflective
- Often arranged by date (reverse chronological order)
- Mixed register, sometimes moving between formal and informal styles
- Catchy titles to engage readers
- Due to mode, able to link to related texts on similar topics which support the writer's purpose
- Through comments from other users, blogs can generate discussion and dialogic ongoing interaction with the text (these last two both affordances unique to the genre)

Write like a speech writer

Reading and listening to some examples of great speeches is necessary to really understand what makes them great, and these need to be seen and heard as much as read and analysed on a page. Discussion of the significance of some of these is also potentially relevant; students need to see speeches as writing that has, on occasion, literally changed the world. Not always overnight but by successfully, carefully, articulating something fundamentally important.

Here are some we like to use in our classroom:

- Martin Luther King's I Have A Dream speech
- Atticus Finch's closing argument in *To Kill A Mockingbird*
- Sajid Javid's 2019 speech on knife crime
- Oprah Winfrey's lifetime achievement acceptance speech at the 2018 Golden Globes

Again, speeches are an area where the use of narrative can aid audience understanding and engagement, and so understanding narrative structures can help students in creating their own.

Components and structure of a speech 'story'

Possible speech components and structure: Take your audience through a 'story'					
1. Hook	**2. Exposition/ setting**	**3. Rising action/ complication**	**4. Climax**	**5. Falling action/ denouement**	**6. Satisfying ending**
• What will you say to get the audience's attention? • Use a compelling image or story? • Say something powerful or challenging about the issue? • Greet people?	• Give the background – why should your topic matter to people? • What is its history? • Why is this relevant to this particular audience? • This might involve sharing some research data too.	• Establish the fact that this is a burning issue. • What will happen if things don't change? • What is at risk? • What are the potential challenges that might arise?	• What is the most important argument in your favour? • What will draw emotion, engagement and agreement from all people?	• Begin to paint a vision of what can happen if things begin to change – why should the audience be hopeful? • What signs are there that good things are happening?	• What are your solutions to this issue? • What practical things could you like to see happening? • How can people help by changing their behaviours, attitudes or habits?

Principles of rhetoric

We keep coming back to Aristotle, don't we?! We have found that developing an understanding of the principles of 'pathos, ethos, logos' as needs of our audience can help with aiming to include elements within a speech to address each of these needs. Teachers have sometimes, in the search for supportive frameworks for students, attempted to create a framework from 'pathos, logos, ethos' as well. In our opinion, these should be viewed as necessary components to include and can guide questioning around engagement with texts, but students should be taught the flexibility to include these *where* in their piece they see fit. There are similar concerns about using PEE, WHW, and so on as frames which, whilst they do provide a scaffold for students, can also prove restrictive and limiting.

Ethos: 'ethics', connections with society and morality.

Pathos: connected to the emotions.

Logos: logical, rational thought, evidence and reasoning.

Exposure to a range of rhetorical devices is also useful. Although students do not necessarily need to learn the wide range of Greek terminology to be able to write an effective speech, looking at the ways in which rhetoric can enhance argument and providing some tools in order to support them is absolutely beneficial. Look at the appendices for a selection of rhetorical devices.

Editing

As part of consideration of performance, we also need to show students how to edit their speeches.

Once your speech is written, practice performing it.

Time it (several times) – how long is it?

Now cut it down to a five-minute version.

Now, a three-minute version.

Finally, a one-minute version.

Perform each version.

Reflections:

- What could you cut and what was critical to the message?
- How did you adapt the language to save time and highlight key points?

- Did this change the way you deliver the speech (prosody) – pace, dynamics, intensity, intonation and stress?
- How does each version change the listening experience for the audience?
- Which version do you feel was the 'best' one? To what extent does this depend on audience and context?

Performance

Accompanying an understanding of prosodics, we also need to discuss the delivery of speeches as key in the process of creating meaning. The pauses, the stresses, the intonation, the pace – students should study and consider them all. Successful delivery needs modelling, and the process of rehearsal and improvement also needs modelling by an expert (in the classroom, this is likely to be you!).

Write like an academic

In our experience, much of the teaching of academic writing is at paragraph level, due to time constraints. Teachers explicitly teach how to select quotations and evaluate which of these will be the most effective, how to identify features of a writer's craft in a text, how to link (more or less clunkily!) what students know about context into a point that they are making, how to write sentences using relevant terminology and exploring the effects on the reader.

What we are sometimes less good at is how to model writing a whole essay. We teach the components but not the whole. This means when we ask students to write a full essay, they end up stringing together some analytical paragraphs, each on a different point, and this can be lacking a central conceptualised argument and feel incohesive. As teachers, we can feel that we have failed. And to an extent, perhaps we have. Our students may be unaware that an essay is not simply a collection of analytical paragraphs, but that it should be an exploration and evaluation of a central thread, an idea or a concept.

Writing in response to literary texts (especially at GCSE) can be subsidiary to reading, as it does form half of GCSE English language and all of GCSE English literature. Writing can also often be tackled as an afterthought – 'it's time to do some writing now', with a perceived need (or given instruction) to show some 'evidence' in students' books that they have understood this section of *A Christmas Carol*.

As with anything else, essay writing needs to be modelled with examples of good essays. By this we do not necessarily mean the essay your best student wrote on the same question last year, we mean exploring the work of the best essayists (Matthew Arnold style), such as the likes of James Baldwin, Virginia Woolf and George Orwell. This helps students see what the essay as an art form in its own right should be, not just what an essay that successfully meets the criteria of the current GCSE specification might look like (with some argument around whether the assessment framework does support students to effective academic writing!). Being able to write a good essay should be a timeless skill and one that does not matter what specification students are writing for. Essays that accompany literature texts that students are already reading can work well, as the background knowledge is something the students already have, for example William Hazlitt's essays on Shakespeare when studying *Macbeth*, or Zadie Smith's (2023) essay on her historical novel and the spectre of Dickens.

Deconstructing academic writing

Teachers should be clear when teaching essay writing of what actually is required to do this successfully (adapted from Quigley, 2017).

- Display knowledge and understanding of how social and literary contexts influence the writer and their text (including how different audiences may respond to the text across time).
- Display knowledge and understanding of the character, themes and language of the text, making connections and inferences from across the text.
- Display knowledge of the writer's choice of literary devices and genre conventions, based on a wider knowledge of literary history.
- Select, retrieve and interpret evidence (predominantly in the form of quotations).
- Make inferences from that evidence on the writer's vocabulary choices based upon a broad and deep academic vocabulary knowledge.
- Plan and organise an essay into a coherent argument, linking salient points that address the essay question.
- Write with accuracy and clarity, including the use of topic sentences, discourse markers and academic vocabulary, all deployed in an appropriate academic style.

Alongside significant elements of knowledge (form, context – literary, personal and socio-historical, characterisation, plot, the writer's methods), there are many different skills at work here. These therefore need breaking down into components within the classroom to practise individually, otherwise within the limitations of working memory students may spend significant amounts of time selecting the best quotation to support their point and forget they need to also embed this, or to write in an appropriate academic register. Annotations of the text are vital and act as a form of scaffold for students to be able to write analytically.

Planning and redrafting

Planning and redrafting are key aspects of any writing process and so the curriculum must build in time for each of these stages as well as the actual writing. We are aware that we are suggesting that curriculum time needs to include opportunities for rereading as well as rewriting, but we feel that these are vital parts of the subject for students to improve! Equally, the likelihood is that this may be best suited to lesson time as opposed to homework, to ensure the necessary teacher input, as well as focusing students in what can sometimes seem an arbitrary part of the process for some.

Routines and habits can be key to assist students in the writing process.

One simple effective approach to any writing task may be:

- Planning (which could include reading, teaching, questioning, modelling, etc)
- Writing
- Teacher feedback
- Redrafting

Planning is about directing students to collect information from a text, memory, or a combination of both, for example the inclusion of contextual information in a piece of analytical writing.

When students have a clear framework for collecting these ideas this ensures against cognitive overload. The planning stage will require judgements about the amount of teacher input and may take the form of several sequential tasks.

For example:

- Annotating a text (could be done via the I-We-You method)
- Structured group discussion
- Filling in a table
- Collecting ideas on a post-it note
- Collating ideas on a whiteboard
- Discussion and ranking of ideas
- Annotating and discussing an exemplar
- Sharing of success criteria

The planning stage can often be useful to introduce students to the 'big question' (see chapter 1) that they will be considering. Understanding the key learning that they are about to undertake can help contextualise the sequence of tasks that the students will undertake and verbal reminders of this can be useful at each stage.

This could then lead to the independent writing stage, where sentence stems may be available for students. At this point teacher feedback is important, and then redrafting for improvement.

Live modelling and metacognitive talk

We know the impact that metacognitive strategies can have for students. Live modelling of any kind of writing can be a successful approach to take; talking through the process is a necessary part of the process so that students hear and appreciate our thinking. For less experienced teachers, you could practice in advance to ensure the quality of your modelling and you could even discretely copy this model to make it look like fully live modelling if you feel less confident to begin with. Here, a visualiser or interactive whiteboard is once again a key piece of equipment.

Worked examples

Give students the success criteria and allow them to annotate and label examples.

Use of tables as a scaffold

A table can be an effective way of organising students' ideas, allowing them to avoid cognitive overload and they can be created quickly in a lesson or produced in advance. They also allow teachers to guide students' thinking in a focused direction, especially if headings are chosen by teachers and if some columns are pre-populated.

For example, exploring the initial impressions of characters in *Animal Farm*:

Name	Animal	Quotation	Inference

Annotate, add to the table, label an example, have a go, teacher feeds back, improve.

A clear link between these elements of planning and the final product (the writing) is important for students to cement their understanding of the planning to writing transition process. At this stage, it might be useful to provide students with some examples and narrate how the planning steps have allowed this piece of writing to be created.

Key elements in metacognition:

- Sentence starters
- Discussion and thinking time
- Annotations
- Guided practice
- Independent practice
- Redrafting

Text response

As discussed in the section on speech writing, we have had some success with using 'pathos, logos, ethos' as a frame to guide questioning of students in their engagement with and considering their responses to texts however, in our experience these are more useful as broad concepts to apply different layers and levels of construction of meaning rather than intended as a frame or model for how to actually write a paragraph, essay or other academic response.

What's the big idea?

We often find that the current GCSE literature framework, with questions that are intended to be accessible to all students, can prevent students from conceptual approaches to their texts. When asked 'Do you think Piggy is an important character in *Lord of the Flies*', the response (and it's not an unreasonable one) is often simply 'yes', rather than an exploration of how Golding uses Piggy to question ideas about social class, leadership and the inherent nature of evil.

To a GCSE student, this is not what they are being asked, so they answer the more obvious question that is in front of them, even when they know the answer to the more intellectually-demanding, thematic question. Part of planning then needs to include looking at sample GCSE style questions and modelling the type of questions that we as experts bring to it. Metacognitively, this supports students to be able to do this independently for themselves after practise. Exploratory and dialogic talk can support this before moving on to writing [page reference to oracy section].

We have also developed assessment objective (AO) sheets, which you can find in the appendices, as a way of getting students to collate and review their ideas in relation to sections of a whole text recently studied, including relevant context and analysis. Again, with regular practise, this supports students to be able to zoom out from the question to the bigger picture of the writer's context and resulting purpose in creating the text, and then zoom back in to the specific detail of the writer's craft.

Choosing responses and models

Modelling writing

To quote Matthew Arnold, if we design our school curriculum to reflect 'the best of what has been thought and said' *and written*, then surely the best models already exist. Who better to teach students how to craft synecdoche or caricature than Dickens? Who better to demonstrate control over iambic pentameter and blank verse than Shakespeare? Whose prose is more exquisite than F. Scott Fitzgerald's? Who masters allusion better than Margaret Atwood? Who better than to demonstrate how, when and why to reject the constraints of Standard English than John Agard or Sam Selvon? Alex Quigley (2022) also points to ideas of mimicry as a way of learning to perfect one's own craft as a practice going back to classical times; in Ancient Rome, only when learners could demonstrate complete mastery of another's style could they have the freedom to create themselves.

In fact, this is perhaps where students can sometimes struggle with writing. As novices, they need to have models for what good writing looks like before they can be fully creative and free. To be able to write, students need to have also mastered most of the knowledge and skills of reading.

Our students who appear more competent and confident writers are often those who have read more and who have, therefore, subconsciously embedded more knowledge of a wider range of writer's styles, forms, genres and what is typical for these. This process happens naturally for avid readers and often makes them stronger writers. We can't give our students the knowledge gleaned from wide reading during our lesson time (and need to encourage their ongoing wider reading outside the classroom), but by making aspects of writing explicit and overtly concentrating on the process and on stylistics, we can signpost what our avid readers probably haven't realised they have internalised.

Essentially, this comes back to the concept of chunking and automating (from Sweller's cognitive load theory), where the skilled writing happening naturally is in part due to less working memory capacity being taken up by certain tasks, which in some cases could even be using a full stop.

Whether writing analytically or creatively, there are multiple ways to achieve success and so students must be provided with multiple examples of examples. These can include former students' work, the work of peers or examples from past exams. Whilst teachers' pre-prepared models also have value, some students can be more inspired by their peers rather than an 'expert'. Once again, use of a visualiser, interactive whiteboard, or even photocopies can be useful resources for students.

We have also found it effective to alternate between examples by students and adults. For example, a passage by Dickens may be an excellent way of demonstrating his use of semi-colons, but if a student has also used them successfully then it can be constructive and celebratory to share their examples. Students often naturally mimic something they have seen (even subconsciously) as effective in another writer's work. We have, for example, seen students adapting the caricatured speech and ideas of Thomas Gradgrind in Dickens' *Hard Times* to write about their own experiences of education, or apply his description of fog in *Bleak House* to a sweet shop. As teachers, we can also carefully select examples to use in the classroom, and to openly encourage students to mimic specific features as a way of developing this in their own writing.

We have already mentioned that SOLO taxonomy seems to have fallen slightly out of favour in educational circles recently but, as a concept, it supports the idea of the interconnectedness of knowledge and skills, which is of key importance in English. Students need knowledge first to be able to create – knowledge of form, vocabulary, genre, conventions, tropes, characterisation and character development and setting, dialogue and punctuation.

We made the point earlier that many, if not most, written responses to literature in the classroom take the form of critical analytical writing. Clearly, this is a written form and a skill that needs to be practised and perfected, both because it underpins the study of English as an academic subject (and we perhaps need to make more of the academic nature of the subject), and because it forms the basis for examination assessment of English literature in Key Stage 4 and 5.

However, this does not necessarily have to be the case all the time. Students could respond to literature in a different form of writing to an essay. Following the ideas inherent in SOLO, this is only possible when they have embedded their knowledge of the literary text, to be able to use that knowledge to create a new text drawing on the first. It takes more skill and craft from the teacher perhaps to interleave form, and initially more time – the conventions of two forms of communication need to be taught, as well as how to match choices about language in the construction of each type of text. However, the significant broadening of students' schemas and potentially the 'stickiness' of this knowledge has to be a pay-off that has to be worth it.

Suggested ideas:

- Banquo's soliloquy in *Macbeth*
- Editing (and associated editorial notes) and curating their own collection of poetry in response to a particular idea or theme
- Prospero's journal as a coloniser drawing on the travel journals of e.g. Christopher Columbus
- Director's notes on performing a play text being studied
- A lawyer's closing speech to the jury for *The Crucible*

Writing sentences

Coleridge famously defined prose as 'words in their best order' and poetry as 'the best words in their best order'. Whilst his point is valid, why are we not encouraging our students to aim for poetry, in this definition, with every word they write and every time they combine two or more words together to make a sentence? Obviously their newspaper articles need to follow the form and conventions of that genre and aren't actually going to be in rhymed couplets of iambic pentameter, but why not try to write every piece of prose, every sentence, as beautifully as if it were actually poetry? If and when we fail, we'll still have written with some wonderful words in the best order!

Students need explicit instruction in and modelling of writing different forms of sentences, and to consider why, when and how to do each of these.

Students need models for:

- Sentence combining
- Sentence expanding
- Sentence shrinking
- Sentence signposting
- Appositives
- Using adjectives, adverbs and adjectival clauses
- Using prepositional phrases

Take a look at the 'writing great sentences' resource in the appendices.

Rather than go through each of these here, the examples attached delve into this in much more detail. We would also recommend Christopher Youles' excellent Sentence Models for Creative Writing, which has lots of creative ideas for developing students' thinking about how they are constructing sentences creatively in a whole range of different scenarios.

Sometimes sentence construction can be planned to be taught as an explicit strategy on their own ('today we are going to focus on using prepositional phrases class'), but more often teachers need to be confident enough in each of these to be able to spot when and how students' work could benefit from applying one of them. The ability to do this will come from your own writing, from using the examples and being secure in editing processes, all of which are rooted in practise.

Writing: how much or how little?

Lots of writing that takes place in the classroom is at paragraph level. This is largely an expediency of time – editing considerations aside, it is difficult to write a full essay in a single sitting, or a full piece of creative writing. Practice is, therefore, often undertaken on a smaller scale, without often discussing what a full essay actually looks like. Teachers often teach students to write an analytical paragraph and then just string a few of those together. This does not necessarily help students build up the skills to mentally conceive, plan, write, redraft/hone/edit a piece in its finished, polished entirety.

Some research within our own school suggests that this pattern is also replicated across the curriculum – most writing undertaken by secondary students is of paragraph length across all their subjects, despite some work in exams (or the real world!) needing to be of a longer length.

There is also less work done on crafting perfect sentences. There is an assumption that students can write sentences, so the focus needs to be on combining a number of these, all doing different things, into a paragraph, with less explicit teaching on the many ways in which a sentence could be constructed and the associated impact on meaning, nuance, and appropriateness for form and register.

Our focus in our own school has been to take 'write less, but better' as our motto, to slow down and reduce the total output we expect from students. In a unit of work (typically between four and ten weeks), students will produce a single written piece. However, this will be crafted and re-edited several times, with components perfected and polished. Students begin by working towards perfect sentences (www.learningspy.co.uk/english-gcse/art-sentences/), and we then consider how these should be combined and crafted to build towards a whole piece, comprised of paragraphs, with each of these envisioned as a part of a bigger picture.

Writing fluency and media

A key component in the development of writing skills is fluency and, at secondary school, the foundational necessity of physical fluency can be overlooked. On many occasions, we have both said to a student 'oh, your handwriting doesn't matter as long as I can work out what you are saying', and to an extent this is true – we are interested primarily with the content and shaping of what our students write and not its presentation (unless we are analysing language and looking at presentational choices as part of intentional shaping of meaning). However – and we are as guilty of this as many other teachers probably are – this can undermine the significance of the challenge of physical disfluency, and the disconnect between thought and the words that end up on the page.

The media and mode of writing, therefore, also has an impact. Earlier we discussed the research in relation to reading digitally, the same must, therefore, be an equal consideration when it comes to writing. Construction of a typed text is different to construction of a handwritten one. Whilst technology can be crucially important in providing supports and scaffolds to students with particular needs, we think differently when we type compared to with pen in hand.

Handwritten plans for anything begin in a linear fashion and end up with offshoots all over the place; sideways lateral connections that span the page and link backwards and forwards. On a computer, this is not possible and thinking is more linear. Writing is thinking.

Consequently, we are concerned about any proposals to move towards digital assessment of students in both reading and writing without fully comprehensive studies into the impact of reading and writing in this way. The skills work differently depending on the mode. Anecdotally, we have witnessed our own children with writing tasks set as home learning and have heard them verbalise complex and interesting sentences that they have then struggled to type. There is a digital skillset to typing that is different to handwriting, using more and more elaborate brain connectivity than typing does: 'Handwriting requires fine motor control over the fingers, and it forces students to pay attention to what they are doing. Typing, on the other hand, requires mechanical and repetitive movements that trade awareness for speed.' (Van der Weel and Van der Meer, 2023)

Indeed, the writing of this book has primarily taken place digitally however, when we have reached a point where we needed to review our work editorially, it necessitated printing to be able to read on paper and, when stuck with a particularly tricky section, resorted to writing – thinking – with a pen in hand. Composition then, of any kind, is perhaps best done in a handwritten form unless there is an additional need that necessitates typing instead (at the behest of one's SENCO). We have found Sedita's (2019) 'writing rope' – similar to the aforementioned Scarborough reading rope – to be helpful in consideration of the various physical and intellectual knowledge-based strands involved in writing.

Handwriting fluency

Often overlooked in the secondary school, fluency and automaticity in handwriting underpin more creative elements to writing and their absence or lack of development impedes students' progress in writing. Here then are some suggestions to support this:

- Focus on Years 7 and 8 – firstly because students are more likely to be receptive when they first enter secondary school and, secondly, because it has been a focus at primary school and so is merely a continuation of student expectation. Thirdly, and of crucial importance, because it needs to be done at this age while there is still time to improve fluency before handwriting habits become permanent.
- Positive recognition and praise.
- Showcase good examples.
- Model our own handwriting – this could include the difference between what writing looks like when it is done quickly compared with carefully, with focused concentration.
- Opportunities to draft, edit and then produce 'best' pieces, which should also include handwriting as one component of this.
- Reminders of best posture and seating positions for fluency and presentation in writing.
- Encourage use of good quality writing implements: fibre-tipped pens, gel pens and nib pens. Good quality fountain pens that do not leak (although they constantly need refilling, which can be disruptive to classroom routines), but definitely not biros. Obviously, there is a cost implication here but we feel that communication with parents on the merits of certain pens can help, as well as obviously ensuring access to the same equipment for pupil premium students.
- Specific targets for handwriting, for example on formation of the tails of letters.

We also cannot stress enough the importance of liaising with colleagues in the school who have significant experience in this area if you have concerns or need additional support, namely your SEN department.

The teacher as a writer

No doubt we have all heard at least a paraphrasing of the derogatory slur from George Bernard Shaw's *Man and Superman*: 'Those who can, do; those who can't, teach.'

We often model academic writing. We model reading skills. We model what perfect sentences look like. But often we show the final product, which can seem unattainable to students at the beginning. What we should be modelling is the whole writing process, making our own struggles, thinking and decision-making explicit and visible. Especially when it is creative and when it feels out of our comfort zone, and most especially when it is imperfect. To awkwardly paraphrase John Legend, all our perfect imperfections should be on display. Students need to see that *everyone* struggles to write perfectly, that writing is a process of ongoing refinement (and sometimes even when something is 'complete' its author may never view it as 'perfect'). They need to see us struggle for ideas, to write 'badly', to grasp for the right word and have to come back to it later, and also to see how we go about improving that first draft. We need to position ourselves in our students' shoes and struggle alongside them. And perhaps, sometimes, we might even be able to enjoy it!

Of course, this takes lesson time and sometimes you may wish to have worked through the process yourself before the lesson, whilst still showcasing the steps, for expediency.

This feels like a leap of faith and that we are exposing ourselves (after all, we are teachers, not writers) but we see it as essentially important for three reasons. Firstly, it seems inherently unfair to ask our students to do something we are not willing to do ourselves, to make themselves vulnerable in front of their peers if we are not prepared to do the same and show them how to manage this. Secondly, it allows us to understand the difficulties of writing better having experienced it ourselves, which ultimately will lead to better teaching (at least if we apply some metacognition and actively reflect on it ourselves!). Finally, and perhaps most importantly, it normalises writing. It makes the process of creating, editing, redrafting, refining, honing, struggling, every day and universal.

Let us try our own teaching strategies and activities and see how well they work, where we struggle and so where our students might struggle too, where they can be improved, where they are brilliant.

And, just to address the point at the start of this section, we'll see your Shaw and raise you an Aristotle (him again): 'Those who know, do. Those who understand, teach.'

Writing commentaries

At university, and to an extent at A-level (both in language and language and literature combined), writing becomes highly self-reflective, and students of writing at this level are often required to write extensive analytical commentaries of their own pieces. So, why not extend this throughout the secondary classroom as well? We have found it an invaluable tool for three reasons. The first is that more than any other activity, it promotes metacognitive focused reflection on work students have produced themselves, really getting them to consider their intended effect and whether they have successfully achieved this.

Secondly, it often then leads to improved editing and redrafting of the work as a result.

Thirdly, it is actually a way of getting students to practise analytical writing and critical thinking whilst also allowing the original task to be creative. So, if you have been reading our recommendation to carry out less analytical writing in favour of writing a range of other forms with concern, perhaps this is a way of making you feel more comfortable about the amount of practice students could get!

Our longer pieces of extended writing always, therefore, require students to write an accompanying commentary on their own work. We model this for students, in the same way that we model what a good piece of journalism, poem or short story could look like, so they can see what is expected of them.

For example, when our Year 7s read *Treasure Island*, we ask them to write a section recasting Long John Silver as an out-and-out villain (having previously read, discussed and analysed the passage to uncover the layers of ambiguity in Stevenson's description).

It might look like this:

Original	Recast
'under the left shoulder he carried a crutch, which he managed with wonderful dexterity, hopping about upon it like a bird.'	'under the left shoulder he demonstrated his mastery of a crutch, manipulating it with awesome dexterity, prowling about upon it like a leopard.'

Commentary example

I changed the verb 'carried' to 'demonstrated his mastery' because I felt this gave an impression of Long John Silver as powerful and in control. 'Manipulated' here is a synonym for the original 'managed' but gives connotations of duplicity and control. I wanted to introduce the idea of Long John Silver's capacity for deception at the very beginning (whereas Stevenson leaves this for Jim to discover later). I changed the adjective 'wonderful' to 'awesome'. Whilst 'awesome' can sometimes mean amazing or wonderful, it additionally conveys a sense of power in Jim being 'awe-struck'. I also reworked the simile 'hopping about upon it like a bird' to 'prowling about like a leopard' because the image of Silver as a bird in the original makes him seem harmless, as birds are small and delicate. I chose a leopard instead, as leopards are also quick but in addition have connotations of threat, whilst retaining the idea of agility and grace of the original. This will make the reader suspect that Silver has harmful intentions towards Jim, possibly even implying he might play with Jim the way a cat plays with its prey.

It takes a little practice and modelling with students. For students who initially find the process difficult or uncomfortable to write about their own choices, we sometimes suggest that they begin by writing about themselves in the third person, as they would any other writer, or passively: 'the choice of the adjective "awesome" connotes…'; they usually progress quite swiftly to feeling confident moving to more personal analysis of their own choices.

Editing

If as we have said, we want our students to write the best words in the best order, this is only achieved through effective editing. 'Effective' is the operative word here; plenty of self and peer assessment falls down in the classroom without being constructively framed, and not therefore leading to the desired improvement, let alone perfection.

Understanding the real role of an editor is important for students here. Alongside classroom discussion, real editing tasks can help to develop this understanding, so a primary piece of advice is that sufficient time needs to be dedicated to editing, as well as description of editorial process.

One strategy for developing this includes setting editorial tasks that include a component of writing. For example, when we study a unit of poetry with Year 9, their task at the end of the unit is to compile their own mini anthology of poetry (linked by a theme), and then to write their own editorial notes to introduce and explain the collection. This includes some analysis of the poems, as well as a need to discuss authorial contexts and connecting but contrasting exploration of themes. Of course, this needs to be modelled to students initially, so we look at the editor's introductions to several books of poetry as well as the editor's notes we have written ourselves to accompany the unit they have been studying, which helps by contextualising comments on poems that the students are already familiar with. An example of this can be found in the appendices under 'editors notes'.

Getting students to function as editors for themselves as well as others is also a useful way of developing metacognition and self-reflection when it comes to writing, which is not always instinctive and so needs strategies to support. Peer assessment is often not as effective as it has the potential to be for a variety of reasons, including a lack of clarity on task objectives, as well as students being unsure about what advice to give to help another improve (they may find it easier to identify areas to develop, but not what to do about them). We use a strategy that firstly gets students to identify areas within their own work with which they are not yet fully satisfied (task and form criteria are often helpful here), and then asking another student to either write an improvement for them, or to suggest a range of ways in which the original writer could improve it themselves. For example:

Writers:

- In your piece of writing, draw a straight line under one sentence/section that you are proud of, **and**
- highlight a sentence/section that you aren't happy with yet.
- Swap books with your editor.

Editors:

Write a sentence to explain why you also like the line that they underlined, e.g.

- Your use of the three short sentences 'Fire. Screaming. Darkness.' helps to set the scene quickly for the reader and provides a heightened sense of tension, **and**

- Either rewrite the section with the squiggly line or write some advice for them on how to improve it. This needs to be specific, for example:

  'walked' is quite vague, but if you changed this to 'marched' it would give us a sense of the character's purpose in coming here.

Making it real

Students need to perceive that editing is a process undergone by any and every writer, otherwise there can be a danger that they assume that it is because they are not a good enough writer to produce a perfectly polished piece the first time. They need to see that nobody does (as Ernest Hemingway put it so bluntly). There are two ways in which to support this: the first is in modelling your own work and the editing of it. This would involve live modelling writing and, whilst doing so, talking through your thought process as you review words that are not sophisticated enough, or you cut out extraneous material, or re-read for clarity or for purpose or to better suit the audience. The second is to share with students the first drafts of writers they know. This is incredibly powerful when it is a text the students are studying in its final form. For example, Blake's revisions of *London* are really useful for students studying the AQA Power and Conflict anthology. We mentioned *Poems in Progress* earlier, but alongside this are facsimiles of many writer's work and drafts available through the British Library's online collection. It is worth searching online as well for other writers who might not be included in these collections – nothing beats a handwritten page with sections crossed through and evident revisions.

Finally, a discussion of what students might be editing *for* is crucial in the classroom. They should be encouraged to re-read and review their own text several times, each time looking at a different aspect:

- Reading for form and genre conventions: does it look and feel like the text it is supposed to be? This might also include presentational elements as well as register.
- Reading for purpose: does the text achieve this? (Again linked to form as well as the task objective students have been given.)
- Reading for audience: this relates to purpose so could be done in conjunction. Does the text influence the audience in the way you intended? For both, a commentary can be invaluable in developing student self-reflection.

- Substituting: focus on lexis. Is every word the best, precisely chosen word? Is there a synonym, and if so, which one works best and why?
- Rearranging: at sentence level, are the words in the best order for the intended effect? What happens if you rearrange them? At text level, is the whole thing structured in the most effective way?
- Editing/trimming: an important part of editing (especially in a professional capacity when work is actually going to be published) is trimming the unnecessary. Is everything you have included necessary? Ask students to justify why. They could also be given a real task where they must remove (for example) 100 extraneous words from their piece. Reflection is important here: which words did they choose to cut and why? How did it affect the overall piece? What if this became 200 words? At what point does the editing down begin to affect their ability to convey meaning?
- Replacing: as part of this trimming process, students could also consider whether they have made the most effective choices, for example could a verb modified by several adverbs simply be substituted for an alternative more precise verb? For example, 'the man walked nonchalantly, aimlessly, feeling carefree' could be changed to 'meandered' or 'ambled'.
- Final review: is every single part of the piece, every word, every piece of punctuation, every literary device, every stylistic choice or choice of form, all designed to make the audience emote?

CHAPTER 6
TEACHING GRAMMAR

The importance of grammar

Alex Quigley is right in our view to talk about giving children the 'gift of grammar'. Given the interplay between language and thought, this is truly an immense gift. Lera Boroditsky's 2018 lecture on this is an excellent way to develop our own knowledge in this area. David Didau (2021c) points out that 'because almost all grammar teaching disappeared from the 1970s onwards, English teachers today have largely managed to muddle through without knowing much.' Whilst we may often enjoy a conversation where one teacher asks another a grammatical point, there is often a hidden undertone of concern that we may not know the answer between us and then how are we going to persuade students that the accuracy of the answer is important. David Crystal (2016) has not only emphasised the need to teach grammar but also highlights the difficulty of bringing the theory behind grammar into practice, which is a key challenge for English departments.

Why grammar matters

In our opinion, grammar matters. It matters because of the need to create clear meaning. It also matters because a really precise understanding of the bones of language allows students, when discussing this sentence from *A Christmas Carol*, 'Oh! But he was a tight-fisted hand at the grindstone, Scrooge; a squeezing, wrenching, grasping, scraping, clutching, covetous old sinner!', to progress their analysis from this:

> 'Dickens uses a list of adjectives to describe how mean and miserly Scrooge is. The list is used to emphasise and exaggerate just how unpleasant Scrooge can be because there are so many adjectives used.'

To this:

> 'Dickens uses a list of participle verbs adjectivally to describe Scrooge. The verbs all have connotations of inflicting pain and suffering on the recipient. As they are dynamic verbs that denote action, this implies that Scrooge is purposefully intending to act

in a miserly way, and conjures up images of him almost literally "squeezing" every last penny out of those who owe him money. This decreases the reader's sympathy for him because he means to inflict pain on to other people, showing his lack of compassion.'

Without unpicking with students whether the list is made up of adjectives or verbs used adjectivally, they are not able to progress their *thinking* to this level of analysis, and that is enabled because of a precise knowledge and understanding of grammar.

Finally, it allows them to master their own craft. Take a look at the section on syntax on page 108 for a demonstration of how this mastery of grammar and syntax can also lead to creativity.

Punctuation and meaning

We know punctuation creates and changes meaning however, we could also ask (as Boroditsky does) whether there is also some interplay between punctuation and thought? In a recent assessment, we asked students to punctuate the sentence 'a woman without her man is nothing' to demonstrate their understanding of how to accurately use a colon, which returned some interesting results. Female students were much more likely to punctuate the sentence in the only way in which a colon can be used grammatically correctly, i.e. 'a woman: without her, man is nothing'. There was nothing to indicate that male students had less grasp as a body of people about accurate application of the colon, so does this imply an unwillingness of those students to accept the implication of the repunctuated sentence? We took from this a mental note that we should not bring issues around gender equality into punctuation in future, even when intended humorously, and that perhaps there's a huge linguistics research project in this!

Lynne Truss's well-known joke about a panda on the back cover of her 2004 book *Eats Shoots and Leaves* provides a convenient way for English teachers to emphasise that grammar equates to (implied) meaning, but teachers are still presented with three key challenges around teaching it:

- Why do people find learning grammar boring?
- What can be done about that in the classroom?
- Is the English department (alongside MFL) responsible for teaching grammar in schools?

We'll address this final point first: who is, and who should be, responsible for teaching grammar in secondary schools?

We would argue that, although the English and MFL departments have significant opportunities and expertise to teach grammar – and an understanding of what is learned when in each subject can help build students' schemas – the disciplinary nature of literacy in secondary schools means that grammar and syntax (as much as vocabulary, reading skills and how to write) all should be taught within the disciplinary frame of each subject. To write effectively in history, students need to be able to master the passive voice, which they are less likely to encounter frequently in English. Similarly, the use of nominalisation in science is a key feature of literacy in that subject, and science teachers who understand the micro rules of communication in science are best placed to support students with how to (for example) nominalise. However, as with everything in the teaching of English, the better students become in the specifics of disciplinary literacy within English, the more they will be able to access across the curriculum as well (revisiting Cox's cross-curricular view).

Challenges for teachers

Ultimately, as already mentioned, a large part of the challenge comes down to the varying teaching of grammar over the last 40 years. Many teachers have a substantive gap in their knowledge when it comes to grammar as they were never taught this explicitly themselves. This can lead to a lack of confidence in teaching it, as well as sometimes a complacency about 'well I managed fine and got my first in English without ever needing to know what an adjective was'. Anecdotally, at least, a higher percentage of English teachers would appear to be literature specialists rather than linguists, meaning they are less likely to have learned much grammar themselves.

Personal CPD is important here. In our department we have conducted a (self-assessed) audit of teacher confidence in being able to accurately explain elements of grammar using the Key Stage 2 national curriculum appendices. The self-assessment element and focus on confidence in explaining rather than own understanding helped to diffuse some of the tension in staff's self-perception of being 'rubbish at grammar' (in a department where we also have several specialists who teach language at A-level and have studied linguistics and language across time at degree level themselves). We would recommend some further detailed reading for teachers, namely Alison Ross's *English Language Knowledge for*

Secondary Teachers, which is excellent in clearly and simply explaining the grammar we need to be able to understand, as well as Jennifer Webb and Marco Giovanelli's *Essential Grammar* that focuses on ways to teach grammar. We do also have some further suggestions of our own to add as well, which you will find further along in the chapter.

Grammar drills

As mentioned in chapter 4, grammar starters can act as a form of retrieval practice at the beginning of a lesson or at key moments within it. Sequenced over time, students can be provided with the benefit of interleaved and spaced practice to become more fluent with particular rules, such as punctuation use, use of Standard English and tenses, for example.

The challenge for teachers is when to teach, or reteach, these rules. Consideration of Rosenshine, once again, would suggest that time needs to be given to clear explanations and models of these rules. There is also a difference in focus between primary and secondary phases – clauses and sentence construction are prioritised at primary level but are not then as significant a focus at secondary, and so this difference needs to be signposted for students.

There are also potential issues surrounding recalling rules to the working memory; grammar learned at primary school might be in a student's schema, but without regular access, our Year 10s look blankly when we ask what kind of adjective 'biggest' is.

Knowledge v application

As part of this discussion, we would observe that often when English teachers assess students' ability to accurately identify the correct definition for a noun, for example, they are able to do so. However, when presented with a sentence, those same students are not able to identify the word functioning as a noun within that sentence. We can be surprised by this and repeat a retrieval task asking students to identify the correct definition for a noun, they do so, and so we move on because it looks like they know the information. Knowing that a verb's function in a sentence is to describe an action or state does not mean that students can accurately identify the verb in 'a rolling stone gathers no moss'. Often they will identify 'rolling' as the verb because sometimes it is used as a verb however, here it is being used adjectivally.

A common (and accurate) language for grammar

Whilst we are on the topic then, a shared and accurate language for identifying word classes is essential. Observing that a 'verb is a doing word' does not help students' understanding when they need to identify the function of stative verbs in a sentence, and they can misidentify 'love' or 'hope' as nouns. There is a further complication in that words can change their function. Love can be a verb, as in 'I love chocolate', but it can also be a noun in 'my love for chocolate is unparalleled'. It causes confusion when they look at Macbeth:

Malcolm	Dispute it like a man.
Macduff	I shall do so,
	But I must also feel it as a man.

'Man' in the dialogue functions as a noun, but then in the subsequent student discussion, 'Malcolm tells Macduff to man up', 'man' functions as a verb. However, it could equally be an adjective if the same student were to talk of someone suffering from 'man flu'!

Rather than providing (inaccurate) absolutes, such as 'love is a noun', we should be asking students what function a word is serving in a sentence. This makes them focus more precisely on exactly how the word is being used in this context and helps them to develop an understanding of the flexibility and fluidity of grammar beyond a few over-simplified rules.

We suggest the following as a starting point:

- A noun's function in a sentence is to denote people, places, objects.
- A verb's function in a sentence is to denote actions or states of being; these include dynamic, stative, modal, imperative and auxiliary.
- An adjective's function in a sentence is to modify or qualify a noun.
- A preposition's function in a sentence is to show direction, time, place, location, spatial relationships, or to introduce an object.
- A pronoun's function in a sentence is to stand in for a noun, but they can also be used to identify possession, or as interrogatives or declaratives (which then needs further unpicking with students!).
- The function of an adverb in a sentence is to provide context by describing how, when, where and to what extent something occurs. They can not only modify verbs but also adjectives and other adverbs.

While we are on the subject, secondary teachers sometimes find themselves combating inaccurate terms for grammar which are 'sticky', such as 'bossy verbs'. We would advocate for just teaching students the full accurate terms for grammar (and everything else) from the outset. A child, aged seven, who can precisely distinguish between 20 different types of dinosaur with Latinate names – or correct their English teacher parent, who has incorrectly identified an animal at a safari park as 'some kind of racoon', that 'obviously it's a binturong' – is perfectly capable of learning 'imperative' to accompany their understanding of the form of a verb used for issuing instructions. Let's not downplay the ability of our students to learn, understand and apply complex, sophisticated terminology because of our own inadequacies in explaining it (or possibly even understanding for ourselves).

Grammar in context

We would, therefore, argue that in order to aid understanding of the fluid ways in which grammar operates as well as the skill required in applying knowledge, grammar is often best taught in context with a full explanation of the relevant grammatical rule or operation.

As part of our curriculum, we have moved towards the teaching and review of grammar largely in the context of a text being taught. The whole department has worked to create grammar starter tasks that relate to specific sections of texts that we teach, which seems to have proven more successful in getting students to understand the significance of a writer's grammatical choices than using grammar drills, which are not in context and are sometimes also only focused on understanding definitions rather than identifying examples within a text. Interestingly, the questions asked do seem to lead students to independently choosing to comment on aspects of grammar and syntax when they are given freedom to select elements of a text to analyse themselves. Some examples of these grammar activities can be found in the appendices under 'GCSE grammar starter'.

Retrieval and application tasks

Take a section of a text you are reading and ask students to label word classes, as fully and precisely as possible. For example, 'first person singular possessive pronoun' should receive more recognition than simply 'pronoun', even though the second answer is not inaccurate.

Do this frequently. You will learn a lot.

Only connect

Particularly with colleagues in the languages department, it is enormously useful to see the curriculum overview for learning the grammar of foreign languages, as often this supports and underlines any corresponding teaching in English. In fact, the grammatical knowledge of many English teachers who have missed out on formal grammar education themselves is derived from their learning of grammatical structures in other languages, reflectively applied to English. Being able to point students to what they already know about conjugating verbs in Spanish or discussing past, present and future tenses in French actually boosts the grammatical schema of students, making the learning more 'sticky'.

Syntax

We cannot discuss grammar without discussing syntactic construction alongside this. That Coleridge quotation from earlier comes to the fore here: 'poetry is the best words in the best order'. Students need to consider the impact of their (and other writers') syntactical choices. Again, teaching syntax in context has some merit, especially with more figurative and poetic texts. Helping students to understand that – specifically when writing some forms such as poetry – writers can and do break what they have been taught are the 'rules' of syntax is important. However, this must be with a proviso that they themselves do have to follow those rules when writing in certain forms and contexts – the Standard English debate is not one to have here!

Rearrange rearrange, rearrange

We have found it is sometimes necessary to demonstrate to students how to rearrange the words they have in front of them into a sentence that makes greater sense. When asked the question 'what have the witches done to the woman's husband?' in Act 1 Scene 3 of *Macbeth*, Year 11 were completely stumped by the location of the verb in the line 'her husband's to Aleppo gone', and were unable to answer the question until it was rewritten on the board as 'her husband's gone to Aleppo'.

In a similar vein, when teaching a reading lesson on skimming and scanning, when students were asked what Bill Bryson's (1995) view of Blackpool was from the following extract, the response from some was 'amazing'. Obviously there is a consideration here of reading multiple times and for tone, part of the point was to look at what detail is missed when we skim/scan texts and only pick out the occasional word that we ascribe importance to. Delving deeper into Bryson's complex syntactical construction, and rearranging this for students, helped them to understand how the syntax initially leads them down one avenue before then bringing them round to his actual meaning.

> Blackpool – and I don't care how many times you hear this, it never stops being amazing – attracts more visitors every year than Greece and has more holiday beds than the whole of Portugal. It consumes more chips per capita than anywhere else on the planet. (It gets through forty acres of potatoes a day.) It has the largest concentration of roller-coasters in Europe. It has the continent's second most popular tourist attraction, the forty-two-acre Pleasure Beach, whose 6.5 million annual visitors are exceeded in number only by those going to the Vatican. It has the most famous illuminations. And on Friday and Saturday nights it has more public toilets than anywhere else in Britain; elsewhere they call them doorways.

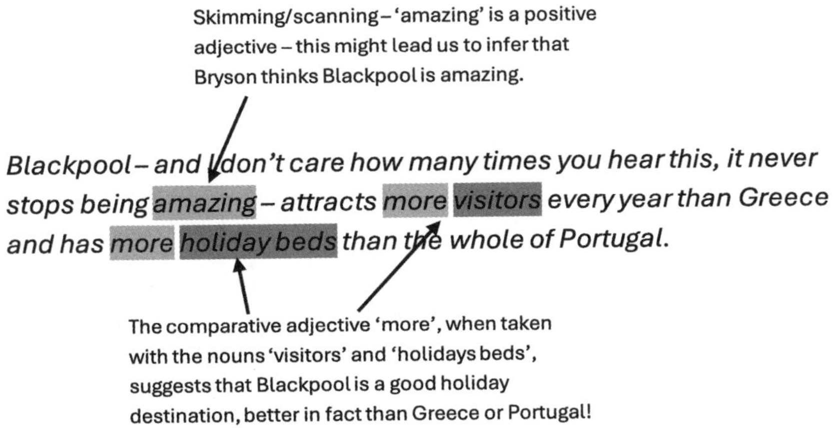

▲ **Figure 7 Annotated sentence**

This complex sentence construction means if we don't read this carefully, we completely miss the point and think the opposite of what Bryson is actually saying.

> It never ceases to amaze me that Blackpool attracts more visitors every year than Greece and has more holiday beds than the whole of Portugal.

What happens when we reorder the sentence? What is the tone of this?

The point really is that students require us to direct and focus their consideration towards syntax. Once they have grasped that meaning can be shaped by where a writer chooses to place words within a sentence (for those words where there is some element of freedom and choice), this is also a choice they can make in their own writing. For example, they could be given a few variations of a sentence and asked which sentence places most focus on the actions of the person? Which seems most sinister? Why? How does rearranging the clauses change or emphasise the tone?

> He watched in the night street, shielded from view.
>
> In the night street, he watched, shielded from view.
>
> In the night street, shielded from view, he watched.

We could use an example like the following one to show students how to improve their own writing – using syntax eventually to shift meaning (this has been worked backwards from the original, which is from a Bob Dylan song Ballad of Hollis Brown).

Initial sentence:	A dog barked outside.
Teacher input:	Change the noun to a more precise one.
Revision:	A coyote barked outside.
Teacher input:	Add an adjective so we now have an expanded noun phrase.
Revision:	A cold coyote barked outside.
Teacher input:	What about the verb? Could you change this to something else, perhaps including a literary device? Is the tense of the verb right? Present tense might feel more immediate.
Revision:	A cold coyote calls outside.
Teacher input:	What about the preposition? Could you change that to a prepositional phrase?
Revision:	A cold coyote calls way out in the wilderness.
Teacher input:	Now if you change the syntax and the order of your clauses here, you could actually use your prepositional phrase to hint at the reason for the coyote calling.
Final version:	'Way out in the wilderness, a cold coyote calls.' (Dylan, 1964)

As with so many things in the English classroom, many opportunities for exploring syntax occur spontaneously. So there is a need for teachers to be alert to opportune moments to explore the effects of changing syntax within students' own writing, as well as contextualised explanation and practice.

CHAPTER 7
TEACHING 'DIFFICULT' TEXTS

The immediate question that needs to be asked here is why are they difficult? What makes a text regarded as 'difficult'? A text might be regarded as 'difficult' for a range of reasons, which can be reduced to:

- Texts that are inherently challenging in their form, language, contexts.
- Texts that are challenging in their ideas (approach to race, sexuality, sex itself).

We suggest different approaches to selecting and teaching these.

Inherently challenging texts

'Shakespeare is so hard.'

'Chaucer's an A-level text.'

Many of us have probably heard similar comments in our teaching careers. It is undisputed that some texts will be harder to read than others. Does that mean we should, therefore, steer clear of them in the classroom? In the Year 7 classroom? Before A-level? In our opinion, categorically no, because then we might be depriving students of some of the greatest works in the English language. The question then is how do we adapt our teaching to allow students to access these complex texts and the richness they bring? An understanding of what the specific complexities of any text are needs to be the starting point. For example, Shakespeare is complex in needing to understand its contextual background; it is rich in figurative language so literal meanings must be teased out; it requires knowledge of poetic form, language, convention and iambic pentameter that, by extension, also make it syntactically complex. Each of these components need to be broken down into layers for students.

Tennent's (2014) 100-point reading indicator can also be useful in judging the complexity of texts.

- Difficult words
  - Language features: does the text contain unique metaphors or imagery, complex sentence structures of multiple clauses and/or rarer items of punctuation?
  - Concepts: how many different ideas and concepts are evoked by the text? These interact with difficult words.

This 'ready reckoner' can be applied to texts in 100-word sections, attributing points to each difficult piece of vocabulary, language feature or concept, and then deduct the total from 100.

95–100 points = text is not difficult to comprehend.

90–95 points = text offers an appropriate degree of challenge.

Fewer than 90 points = text may be difficult for some pupils to read independently.

This does not mean that texts scoring under 90 points should be avoided but, simply, that they will require further scaffolding by the teacher in the classroom to enable students to comprehend (and should probably not be given to students without this level of support). We have already discussed strategies for helping with complex syntax and explicit vocabulary instruction above. As part of this, there are also times when teachers need to promote 'it's ok to not understand every word', whilst still maintaining student effort and specific strategies for trying to decode.

In terms of difficult concepts, this is often a question of how to make these universal and relatable. Pairing texts can help student perception of literature as an ongoing cultural dialogue across time, for example reading parts of Chaucer's *Canterbury Tales* and (carefully selected for expletive reasons!) extracts from Patience Agbabi's reworking Telling Tales; matching *The Strange Case of Dr Jekyll and Mr Hyde* with Edgar Allan Poe and scripts from *Wednesday* to look at the use and adaptation of Gothic tropes across time and space; or *Nineteen Eighty Four* alongside *The Last of Us* (or any other age-appropriate dystopian TV series). Modern adaptations are likely to have a greater level of immediate relatability but will also help to encourage an idea that this dialogue across time makes older texts still relevant.

Challenging ideas

'Othello? With Year 7? Are you serious?'

Our view is yes! Because we're going to focus on racism and jealousy, not the sex! We should not shy away from teaching texts with challenging ideas: of course, understanding the context of your setting's intake and individual students is important, but we believe that this is part of teaching English.

Offensive language and swearing

This needs to be nuanced. Certainly, almost all our students have encountered language in their lives that some might deem to be offensive in the form of swearing for emphasis (with expletives often used adjectivally). Tackling this is a rather different kettle of fish compared with use of language that is intended to be derogatory and hurtful around protected characteristics or diversity.

Swearing can be relatively easily prefaced in the classroom with 'spoilers' to warn what is coming and to give students an opportunity to indicate if they would prefer to opt out of an activity (they almost never do!) due to the bad language. This allows teachers to tackle the appropriateness of language use, to discuss how and why swear words might be used for effect (after all this type of analysis and consideration is fundamental to English), and in what contexts it is and is not acceptable, but also to mitigate caregiver concerns about what their child is being exposed to.

There is also scope to consider language evolution over time when it comes to acceptability of swearing. This kind of consideration is particularly relevant at A-level. For example, if students are studying Carol Ann Duffy at A-level then it is essential, or linguistics study in either A-level language or language and literature combined. We have found the following *Guardian* articles interesting to discuss in the classroom (and also provide some additional exposure to some opinion-type journalism):

'Swearing is becoming more widely acceptable, linguistics experts claim' (David Batty, The Guardian, 6 January 2024)

'It's s****ing big and it's ***ing clever: why swearing makes you fitter, happier and more persusasive' (The Guardian, 1 November 2022)

Using the 'n' word (and similar)

This is a really tricky area. On one hand, we feel it is incredibly important to tackle inappropriate and offensive language head on. On the other hand, reading materials in class that contain language that could be regarded as offensive or abusive in certain contexts has to be handled with delicacy and nuance. This is not always an easy thing for a teacher to feel comfortable with, especially depending on the cohort of students in front of you. Intentionally introducing this debate through text choice might feel a bit like making a rod for our own backs; if it works, then this is brilliant and we are effectively combating racist, homophobic or gendered abuse. However, our concerns are around what happens if it were to go wrong. This could potentially do more damage than not having the conversation at all.

Lucy wanted to include Dean Atta's fabulous poem *I am Nobody's Nigger*, written in response to the murder of Stephen Lawrence, in a scheme of poetry for Year 9, as Atta's eloquent exposition of why the word cannot and should never be appropriated by anyone, of any race, explains the issue better and more personally than we felt that we could. But what if they just don't get it? In the end, we opted for other texts by a diverse range of writers who discuss ideas about race and racism openly but without using language that in itself might be problematic in the classroom. We are still having the conversation but curating the words for that dialogue carefully.

Perhaps with certain groups of students, with a high level of sensitivity, it is possible.

Of course, it is vital to point out here that teaching a text that includes the 'n' word is not a toleration of racism at all. Racism, just like other protected characteristics, has no place in society and we should be able to help students find facts about these and the law, and as educators we need to consider how to offer pupils a balanced account.

CHAPTER 8
FEEDBACK/FEEDFORWARD

This is always a huge topic of concern for teachers, but it is especially one for English teachers. The work we assess, if it is work that has any real meaning in terms of measuring our students' ability in our subject, necessarily has enormous variety, and we are attempting to apply a set of objective criteria to something that is fundamentally subjective. Is one student's ability to craft rich figurative language 'better' than another student's sparse prose with a really creative structural feature? How can we pitch these things against one another? And then any advice and guidance we give students on how to improve this piece of work is, and must be, as individualised as the work itself and therefore is incredibly time consuming if it is to be of any value.

Good feedback practice:

1. Facilitates the development of self-assessment (reflection) in learning.
2. Encourages teacher and peer dialogue around learning.
3. Helps clarify what good performance is (goals, criteria, expected standards).
4. Provides opportunities to close the gap between current and desired performance.
5. Delivers high quality information to students about their learning.
6. Encourages positive motivational beliefs and self-esteem.
7. Provides information to teachers that can be used to help shape the teachings. (Nicol and McFarlane, 2006)

Feedforward

Dylan William's view of feedback is that 'the focus of well-timed feedback should be to move learning forward' (Education Endowment Foundation, 2021b). However, at times, there can be a danger within teaching that feedback becomes backwards looking, focusing on assessing the work students have produced and then advising about how this piece of work that has already been completed by the student could have been done better. William also reminds us that the key idea is that 'after feedback, students will be able to do better at some point in the future on tasks they have not yet attempted', and that 'the only thing that matters with feedback is what learners do with it'.

In our department, we have moved to more of a 'feedforward' model for pieces of work; students receive more input and feedback from their teachers before they complete a significant piece of written work rather than after. We also allow students to use notes, plans and to redraft earlier work, rather than springing a totally unseen assessed piece on them. Typically, in writing in the real world, processes of redrafting, editing, reflection, feedback and input from others produces a better piece over time. However, the current examination system requires students to output work in time-constrained conditions. Whilst this is something we are working towards, if our focus is on how students can become better writers, this means we need to adapt our ways of assessing and providing feedback on work in order to build those skills, rather than replicating exam conditions and hoping that giving feedback afterwards will help students learn how to write better. Our guiding vision is that if the ultimate aim is to improve student work, then the final piece should be a reflection of the best they are able to produce.

Practical feedback strategies and resources

Sticker marking/marking grids

Plenty of examples of these exist. You will find resources ('English Language Paper 1 full RAG feedback' and 'Literature feedback mark sheet') in the appendices to some that we have developed.

Feedback method 1

The teacher reads and reviews all student work and simply puts a sticker or writes a simple code (e.g. L3+) in the student's book.

This then corresponds to a marking grid, set of assessment criteria or range of feedback tasks that are recorded centrally somewhere else, either on a sheet given to students or displayed on the board. This focuses your time and effort on reading and considering the work and reduces the amount of writing required in a student's book. (Obviously personalised comments can be included where relevant and necessary in your own judgement.)

Feedback method 2

Marking grids are used which can simply be highlighted or circled to show where students have met certain criteria.

A word in your ear: audio feedback

We have been working recently on delivering audio feedback for GCSE and A-level students on extended writing (literature essays and writing pieces for GCSE English language). We are predominantly using voice notes recording apps on mobile devices and tablets to simply record our verbal comments on student's work, in a similar way to how we would make suggestions for improvement and identify areas of good performance in the classroom. The idea is that this is a more dialogic form of feedback and can increase efficiency as we speak a number of times faster than we can write, so we are able to provide more detailed and personalised feedback to students on a piece of work.

Aside from potential issues with technology, there is also a considerable need when recording one's own voice to be careful with prosodics as students do not have any facial expressions to accompany the sound of your voice, so it is important to be mindful of pitch and intonation.

In our experience, audio feedback does nothing to reduce time spent on feedback or increase efficiency. What it does do though is provide better feedback, and if this can be achieved in the same amount of time as less efficient written comments then, in our view, this is worth exploring as an option.

The administration of delivering this to students through technology is an additional layer of time as files must be transferred. For safeguarding reasons, we would recommend doing this through school computer systems (email, Teams messages, etc) to ensure all communication is through appropriate, professional and licensed channels.

As with any skill in teaching, it takes time to become truly effective at delivering feedback verbally and recording it, so teachers need to be prepared to invest time, have patience and particularly to be reflective about their own teaching practice, looking for improvements.

CHAPTER 9
ENJOYING AND PROMOTING ENGLISH

Culture capital

So many children do not have the rich experiences of cultural capital that Pierre Bourdieu describes as 'help[ing] us navigate culture and alters our experiences and the opportunities available to us'. Sam can give an example of a past GCSE English language paper that included a description of Oxford Circus in it. Using this as a Year 10 exam paper, one student referred to Oxford Circus in their answers numerous times however, their understanding of it being an actual circus rather than a bustling junction in London of course impacted their answers.

One of the joys of English – not necessarily just fiction, but non-fiction also – is the ability to transport readers to places and experiences that they would never have been to before. As mentioned previously, there are huge decisions to make in terms of curriculum and its diversity and it is so important that we try our best to provide students with the widest possible experiences that we can offer: in short, the Hinterland (Counsell 2022) that was introduced in the opening chapter. Our curriculum should be designed to increase the cultural capital of students whilst also acknowledging the limitations of time which does not allow us to 'do it all'. The suggestions in the sections below on enjoyment of and promoting English have some additional ways in which this could also be worked towards.

Enjoying English

This is an important section with some key tips on how to get the kids to enjoy what they do.

Value and success

Students will often tell us that they enjoy subjects that they value and feel successful at (we are ignoring the impact of favourite teachers here!). While everything in this book is aimed at student progress and success, we really would like to hope that these elements also bring enjoyment to students. Consideration of text choice is important, but we also feel it is incumbent on the teacher to make any text relevant to our students.

Students appreciate clear communication and scaffolding that allows them to interpret meanings. If, as classroom practitioners, we can teach effectively to aid student progress, our students may also begin to enjoy English as they perceive they are getting better at it. We are sure that every English teacher can give cherished examples of students who battled with the subject but also leave Year 11 telling us that they have started to read books for enjoyment.

Extra-curricular

There is such a wide range of extra-curricular activities that can be linked to English. Let's not forget that these do not solely have to be within the domain of English teachers and that we should celebrate and encourage colleagues from other subjects being involved in these too!

Examples can include:

- Book club: students enjoy an informal discussion about books without the need for written analysis, possibly aimed at a particular key stage.
- Creative writing: this could have a focus, say poetry, or the focus could change periodically.
- Drama club: neither of us would claim to be the experts compared to our drama-teaching colleagues, but what better way to bring a text to life for students?
- Debating club and public speaking: there are often inter-school and other competitions related to this. Many local Rotary Clubs run the 'Youth Speaks' competition that we have found to be an invaluable and enjoyable experience for our own students.
- Journalism club: school newsletters, but journalism can also reach further than this.
- Connect with your local university's English/media/communication department (and help to maintain these): many universities have school outreach programmes that offer experiences in a whole range of areas, including journalism and writing competitions for school students, as well as sometimes exposure to 'academic university' English. This is no bad thing, as it can often be more creative and exciting than English at Key Stage 4!

Workshops and writing clubs can also validate other forms of communication that tend to be less studied in the classroom, for example graphic novels, which could be looked at in conjunction with colleagues in art.

Promoting English: 'Only connect'

Hopefully our view of the fundamental, essential importance of English has become clear over the pages of this book, its significance in helping to navigate the world, in self-development and empathy, in the ability to articulate and communicate whatever ideas and emotions we need to.

We have also identified it as a subject under threat, perhaps continually since arguments about what English even 'is' have perpetuated since it has been conceived of as an academic subject in its own right. Hopefully the previous few sections have also highlighted some areas in which classroom teachers can have meaningful and long-lasting impact in addressing these threats and showcasing the value of our subject, not only in terms of its usefulness to other subjects or leading to successful careers but also in being able to see, share, appreciate, understand and navigate all of those things that have no monetary 'value' but are still essential parts of human existence, such as joy, beauty, friendship, happiness, sorrow, pain, suffering, loss.

Collaboration: the SHAPE of things to come?

Undoubtedly, the acronym STEM has been enormously successful as a shortcut for certain subjects and to promote their value at a time when there were concerns about insufficient numbers of people studying STEM-related subjects to fulfil the requirements of the workforce. We do not wish to undermine the importance of STEM subjects either; young people should experience an extensive and varied curriculum with depth in order to develop a full understanding of the world around them and to be able to value their own skills and interests, wherever those may take them. Plus, we will always need scientists, engineers, accountants and doctors in the world! However, a narrative perpetuated in part by governments, the media and caregivers has led in some areas to a perception that only STEM subjects have any value in the marketplace for students' future careers and they are penalising themselves (financially, at least) in a modern capitalist world if they choose to study anything else.

To challenge some misconceptions around the value of the arts, humanities and social sciences (both intrinsic and also in terms of economics and careers), the British Academy has come up with the acronym SHAPE[1] to complement STEM as a way of grouping non-STEM subjects together. The idea of SHAPE is around 'Connected Knowledge'. While much of the work of the British Academy is looking at learning and research in so-called SHAPE subjects at university and beyond, we feel that the concept of SHAPE has some merit in the secondary school in promoting SHAPE subjects together, in collaboration, across the school.

In his 1910 novel *Howard's End*, E. M. Forster called on us to 'only connect the prose and the passion, and both will be exalted'. So, let's connect.

What this might look like in practice

Coordinate curriculums

While the idea of a whole school interleaved secondary curriculum across subjects sounds like a metacognitive utopia, it is also likely to be impractical, unwieldy and potentially would not allow individual subjects to explore areas they need to within their own disciplines if everything had to be tied to a centralised curriculum. However, there is value in being aware of what is taught at any time in other subjects as this allows teachers to draw out the connections that exist between English and history, art, music, drama, politics, psychology, geography. The nature of cultural capital in English means that a broad (if not deep) understanding of all of these subjects helps English teachers, so it stands to reason that making those connections will also help our students. This can work both ways as, for example, the role of the historian is to search for balanced and objective understandings, so the human experience conveyed by texts read in English can help history students understand the individual and personal impact of events they study. And so on.

It would be (and is, because we have done it) a relatively straightforward task to look at the curriculum maps of other subjects, perhaps to discuss curriculum sequencing with subject leads in other areas, and to add a brief summary of this into our own curriculum maps for English. This would give teachers something to use as reference and therefore connect learning in different subjects for students at the relevant time.

1 Social sciences, humanities and the arts for people and the economy – it probably benefits from the snappier acronym!

SHAPE days

Many schools facilitate STEM related careers days. So why not do the same for SHAPE?

This might look slightly different, so rather than or in addition to having speakers visit for certain jobs, plan a day of activities that help students to see how the skills and knowledge from each of their subjects interconnect in real world situations. There is obviously a significant time factor in organising this. We have found our colleagues in all SHAPE subjects across the school are very keen to get involved and support as their recruitment for A-level, and often also GCSE, is under a similar threat to English.

For example, a 'politics game' could bring in geography, politics, English (in terms of diplomacy and negotiation, developing oral skills), foreign languages and DT to ask students to represent different fictitious countries in a real world negotiation. This scenario could require practical design and engineering solutions (such as planning and negotiating the location of a proposed bridge between countries), as well as a need to understand and preserve each other's cultures, traditions and heritages – set up to be partially in conflict with each other. This would serve to highlight the inherent value of each subject's potential and necessary contribution to real world challenges. It could also be accompanied by tasks looking at a sustainable fashion and food collaboration between DT and geography, potentially using English skills to advertise and market, as well as a cultural celebratory showcase (developed by music, art, English and drama), and perhaps some student journalism running alongside the entire day to document and report on what has been taking place.

Careers in the curriculum

Make the case for English in supporting careers obvious, and where possible, overtly connected to the English curriculum. For example, when studying poetry, talk about being a poet with some real-world valuable information about how you might actually be a poet. Visiting writers into school can also help with this – ask them to share their own career journeys. Similarly, when reading a newspaper article, talk in real terms about the path to becoming a journalist.

It's important to think creatively here: if you need to be able to read people, to negotiate and communicate exceptionally well as a hostage negotiator, what could help you acquire the necessary skills better than

English? The British Academy's (2020) 'Qualified for the Future' report has some useful statistics that are great to share with students. As well as discussing what skills and abilities employers are actually looking for in prospective employees and how SHAPE subjects can build these, the very process acts as proof that English helps to build and evaluate evidence and critical thinking skills as part of an argument!

We would like to finish this book with a call to arms. While perhaps the question of what English is and what it is for has always been an inherent aspect of the subject,[2] it is more pertinent than ever before and as English teachers we need to take a stand on what we believe English can and should be. If there is a narrative that STEM subjects are more 'valuable' for society or for individual career development, let us question what values are being discussed and present options and choice.

We can take back control of this narrative and more openly tell our story of why English matters in our own way. We are not talking for a moment here about devaluing any other subject. There is a necessary and vital place in the world for architects, engineers, doctors, nurses, radiographers and accountants, just as there is a place for musicians, interior designers, writers, politicians and poets. If we do not help our students to make the best choice for them then we are failing as educators. We simply need to insert another voice into the narrative that advocates for the students who love English and don't know what they want to do as a career yet. We need to be a voice for the writers, the dreamers, the ones who are told 'journalism is too risky but accountancy is a stable job' or 'you can write in your free time, no one ever made a living out of writing' (and perhaps there is some element of truth in this, but economic equity for artists is a matter to discuss elsewhere), or even 'what are you going to do with that, be an English teacher?'

If English is about communication and collaboration, let us work with our colleagues in other departments and pastoral leads and those responsible for careers, to discuss how we can help our students to consider all aspects of job (and life) satisfaction, alongside monetary value.

If public examinations do not currently consider the full breadth and potential of what English can be, let's take back control of this. We need to have faith that if we teach our subject the way we want it to be, the way we love it, we will help our students enough that not only will they

2 See David Didau's *Making Meaning in English* for an excellent overview of the history of the teaching of English.

excel in examinations but also they might enjoy English too. They might even learn something about themselves, society, and human existence along the way. This isn't blind faith. As teachers, it is our role to plan for students to develop their ways of thinking in this critical way – we must give thought to aspects like consideration of form as part of curriculum design at a high level to ensure that we deliver for our students.

All telling is telling it slant, so here's ours. Go out there and, as English teachers, tell your own truth, and in doing so help your students to find their truth and their voice to shape their own narratives.

BIBLIOGRAPHY

Alexander, R. J. (2013) 'Improving oracy and classroom talk in English schools: achievements and challenges', The University of York, *Primary First*, pp. 22–29.

Ault, A. and Walker, L. (eds) (2022) *Poems in Progress: Drafts from Master Poets*. British Library Publishing.

Batty, D. (2024) 'Swearing is becoming more widely acceptable, linguistics experts claim', *The Guardian*, 6 January. www.theguardian.com/media/2024/jan/06/swearing-is-becoming-more-widely-acceptable-linguistics-experts-claim.

Bennett, T. (2020) *Running the Room: The Teacher's Guide to Behaviour*. John Catt Educational Ltd.

Biggs, J. B. and Collis, K. F. (1982) *Evaluating the Quality of Learning: The SOLO Taxonomy (Structure of the Observed Learning Outcome)*. Academic Press.

Blair, S. (2021) *Orwell's Animal Farm: The Graphic Edition with CSEC Study Guide*. Hodder Education.

Booker, C. (2005) *The Seven Basic Plots: Why We Tell Stories*. Continuum.

Boroditsky, L. (2018) 'How language shapes the way we think', *Open Educational Resources Collection*, 13. www.irl.umsl.edu/oer/13/.

The British Academy (2020) Qualified for the Future: Quantifying demand for arts, humanities and social science skills. https://www.thebritishacademy.ac.uk/documents/1888/Qualified-for-the-Future-Quantifying-demand-for-arts-humanities-social-science-skills.pdf.

Bromley, M. (2017) 'Teaching Practice: Hinge Questions', *SecEd*, 25 January. Retrieved from https://www.sec-ed.co.uk/content/best-practice/teaching-practice-hinge-questions.

Bryson, B. (1995) *Notes from a Small Island*. Doubleday.

Cornerstones Education (2022) 'How to balance knowledge and skills in the primary curriculum', *Cornerstones Education blog*, 22 December. Available at: https://cornerstoneseducation.co.uk/news/how-to-balance-knowledge-and-skills.

Counsell, C. (2018) 'Senior Curriculum Leadership 1: The indirect manifestation of knowledge: (A) curriculum as narrative', *The Dignity of the Thing*, 7 April. Available at: https://thedignityofthethingblog.

wordpress.com/2018/04/07/senior-curriculum-leadership-1-the-indirect-manifestation-of-knowledge-a-curriculum-as-narrative/.

Crystal, D. (2016) 'A defence of grammar', *TES*, 3 June, pp. 26–32.

Delgado, P., Vargas, C., Ackerman, R. and Salmerón, L. (2018) 'Don't throw away your printed books: A meta-analysis on the effects of reading media on reading comprehension', *Educational Research Review*, 2, 23–38.

Department of Education and Science (1989) The Cox Report. London: Her Majesty's Stationery Office.

Didau, D. (2014) 'A simple theory about writing', *Learning Spy*, 23 April. Available at: https://learningspy.co.uk/literacy/theory-writing/.

Didau, D. (2018) 'Why English is not a "skills based" subject', *Learning Spy*, 27 April. https://learningspy.co.uk/featured/why-english-is-not-a-skills-based-subject-2/.

Didau, D. (2019) 'Where we're getting curriculum wrong Part 1: Cultural capital', *Learning Spy*, 11 December. Available at: https://learningspy.co.uk/curriculum/where-were-getting-cultural-capital-wrong/.

Didau, D. (2021a) 'Specifying a concept-led KS3 English Curriculum', *Learning Spy*, 23 October. Available at: https://learningspy.co.uk/assessment/specifying-a-concept-led-ks3-english-curriculum/.

Didau, D. (2021b) 'Telling Better Stories', *Learning Spy*, 21 June. Available at: https://learningspy.co.uk/featured/telling-better-stories/.

Didau, D. (2021c) *Making Meaning in English*. Routledge.

Dylan, B. (1963) *The Ballad of Hollis Brown*. New York: Columbia.

Education Data Lab (no date, a) 'Results day analysis: English literature A-Level', *Education Data Lab*. Available at: https://results.ffteducationdatalab.org.uk/a-level/english-literature.php?v=20230817.

Education Data Lab (no date, b) 'Results day analysis: English language A-Level', *Education Data Lab*. Available at: https://results.ffteducationdatalab.org.uk/a-level/english-language.php?v=20230817.

Education Endowment Foundation (2021a) *Improving Literacy in Secondary Schools*, guidance report, 27 October. Available at: https://educationendowmentfoundation.org.uk/education-evidence/guidance-reports/literacy-ks3-ks4.

Education Endowment Foundation (2021b) *Teacher Feedback to Improve Pupil Learning*, guidance report, 22 October. Available at: https://educationendowmentfoundation.org.uk/education-evidence/guidance-reports/feedback.

Enser, Z. and Enser, M. (2020) *Fiorella & Mayer's Generative Learning in Action.* John Catt Educational Ltd.

Fiorella, L. and Mayer, R. (2015) 'Eight Ways to Promote Generative Learning', *Educational Psychology Review*, 28(4), 717–741.

Frouda, K., Levinson, L., Maddox, C. and Smith, P. (2023) 'Middle-schoolers' reading and processing depth in response to digital and print media: An N400 study',

The Guardian (2022) 'It's s****ing big and it's ***ing clever: why swearing makes you fitter, happier and more persusasive', The Guardian, 1 November. www.theguardian.com/science/2022/nov/01/its-big-and-its-clever-why-swearing-makes-you-fitter-happier-and-more-persuasive.

Hart, B. and Risley, T. R. (1995) Meaningful differences in the everyday experience of young American children. Paul H Brookes Publishing.

Hopkins, E., Asin, S., Cowan, S., McKenzie, C. and Thornborough, J. (2023) *English Studies Provision in UK Higher Education*, The British Academy, June. Available at: https://www.thebritishacademy.ac.uk/publications/english-studies-provision-uk-higher-education/.

Kidd, D. (2018) 'A Rich Curriculum', *Love Learning*, June 11. Available at: https://debra-kidd.com/2018/06/11/a-rich-curriculum/.

Korochkina, M., Marelli, M., Brysbaert, M. and Rastle, K. (2024). 'The Children and Young People's Book Lexicon (CYP-LEX): A large-scale lexical database of books read by children and young people in the United Kingdom, *Quarterly Journal of Experimental Psychology.*

Latham, D. (2002) How Children Learn to Write: Supporting and Developing Children's Writing in Schools. London: Paul Chapman.

Levine, C. (2016) 'Forms, Literary and Social', *Dlibur*, (2).

Lorde, A. (1984) *Sister Outsider: Essays and Speeches.* Crossing Press.

Miller, J., Keary, A. and Windle, J. (2012) 'Assessing the reading and writing of EAL/D students: Issues and implications', *TESOL in Context*, 20(3), 1–15.

Nicol, D. J. and Macfarlane-Dick, D. (2006) 'Formative assessment and self-regulated learning: a model and seven principles of good feedback practice', Studies in Higher Education, 31(2), pp. 199–218.

Nicholls, N. (2022) 'GCSE English Language: Not Fit for Purpose', NATE Teaching English, Issue 29, Summer, pp.16–17.

Quigley, A. (2017), 'How to Train a GCSE Writer' blog in '*The Confident Teacher*', 15 April, 2017. Retrieved from https://www.theconfidentteacher.com/2017/04/how-to-train-a-gcse-essay-writer/ [Accessed 11.01.24]

Quigley, A. (2022) *Closing the Writing Gap*. Routledge.

Pinkett, M. and Roberts, M. (2019) *Boys Don't Try? Rethinking Masculinity in Schools*. Routledge.

Ransome, A. and Hart-Davis, R. (ed.) (1985) *The Autobiography of Arthur Ransome*. Century Publishing.

Rastle, K. (2019) 'The place of morphology in learning to read in English', *Cortex*, 116, 45–54.

Rosenshine, B. (2012) 'Principles of Instruction', *American Educator*, Spring. Available at: https://www.aft.org/sites/default/files/Rosenshine.pdf.

Ross, J. (2020) 'Chapter 1: Write like a short story writer by Jacob Ross' in J. Webb, *Teach Like A Writer*. John Catt Educational Ltd.

Sedita, J. (2019) 'The Strands That Are Woven Into Skilled Writing', www.keystoliteracy.com/wp-content/uploads/2020/02/The-Strands-That-Are-Woven-Into-Skilled-WritingV2.pdf.

Shanahan, T. (2019) 'Five Things Every Teacher Should Know about Vocabulary Instruction', *Shanahan on Literacy*, 28 September. Available at: https://www.shanahanonliteracy.com/blog/five-things-every-teacher-should-know-about-vocabulary-instruction.

Smith, Z. (2023) 'On Killing Charles Dickens', *The New* Yorker, 3 July, https://www.newyorker.com/magazine/2023/07/10/on-killing-charles-dickens.

Stimpson, C. (1990) 'Reading for Love: Canons, Paracanons, and Whistling Jo March', *New Literary History*, 21(4), 956–976.

Sweller, J. (1988) 'Cognitive Load During Problem Solving: Effects on Learning', *Cognitive Science*, 12(2), 257–285.

Tennent, W. (2014) Understanding Reading Comprehension: Processes and Practices. Sage.

Tennyson, A. (1842) 'Ulysses', in A. Tennyson, *Poems*. London: Edward Moxon, Dover Street.

Van der Weel, F. R. and Van der Meer, A. L. H. (2023) 'Handwriting but not typewriting leads to widespread brain connectivity: a high-density EEG study with implications for the classroom', *Frontiers in Psychology*, 14.

Webb, J. (2020) *Teach Like A Writer*. John Catt Educational Ltd.

Westbrook, J., Sutherland, J., Oakhill, J. and Sullivan, S. (2019) 'Just reading: the impact of a faster pace of reading narratives on the comprehension of poorer adolescent readers in English classrooms. University of Sussex. Journal contribution.

Willcox, G. (1982) 'The Feeling Wheel: A Tool for Expanding Awareness of Emotions and Increasing Spontaneity and Intimacy', *Transaction Analysis Journal*, 12(4), 274–276.

Wood, C., Garcia-Salas, M., Schatschneider, C. and Torres-Chavarro, M. (2024) 'Morphological Complexity in Writing: Implications for Writing Quality and Patterns of Change', *American Journal of Speech-Language Pathology*, 33(3), 1432–1442.

World Book Day (2024) 'Judgement and expectations are putting children off reading', *World Book Day*, March. Available at: https://www.worldbookday.com/2024/03/judgement-and-expectations-are-putting-children-off-reading/.

APPENDICES

Use the QR code below to access the appendices and resources referenced throughout this book.

Click on Secondary English in Action to access the menu for the resources.